Out of Ordinal

Kiyoshi Hamada

ISBN Paperback: 979-8-9937169-2-3

TABLE OF CONTENTS

Introduction

Humans begin their lives at birth, with no inheritance of knowledge and wisdom. An infant starts life from zero. Throughout their lives, humans learn from their own experiences and various sources of information, ultimately building wisdom. Individual emotional traits—such as anxiety—affect human behavior. The next generation, however, does not inherit the accumulated knowledge and wisdom and must start all over. This is why human history repeats itself.

Science and technology, on the contrary, accumulate a wealth of knowledge, which humans inherit to advance to a higher level. People benefit from the advancements in science and technology, but these advancements can also be destructive to society. Human behavior depends on how individuals apply the wealth of knowledge during their own lifetimes.

The purpose of life depends on how individuals are valued. Some may find value in secular work, a profession, a hobby, their own business, social work, education, sports, or other pursuits.

Out of Ordinal is the story of a person who was born in Japan and, according to the majority of Japanese, experienced a rather "out-of-ordinal" life in Japan and the United States. He witnessed the prosperity and failure of Toshiba Corp. from its preliminary period to its later years. He remained a lifelong seeker of the relationship between body and soul.

Part I

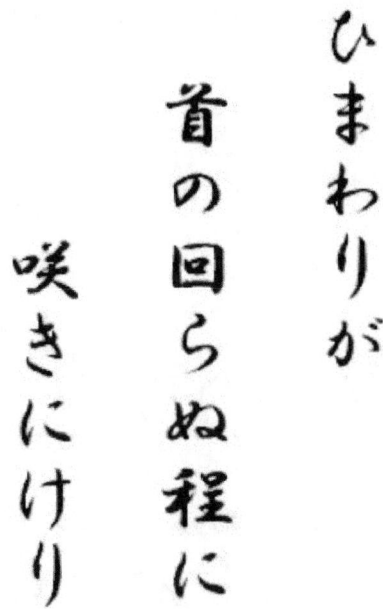

Sunflowers

Hard to turn its' neck

With full blossom

The sunflower bows—
its full-bloomed, heavy blossom
too weighty to lift.

CHAPTER 1
Witnessing Toshiba Corp's Fall from Prosperity to Failure

Prosperity

Toshiba is the oldest electrical/electronic manufacturing company and a pioneer of engineering product development in Japan. The company's predecessor, Tanaka Seizo-sho, founded Japan's first telegraphic equipment plant in Tokyo in July 1875. It grew to become the first electric incandescent lamp plant in 1890 and further expanded to manufacture consumer and industrial electrical/electronic products. The name of the company was changed to Shibaura Engineering Works in 1904, then changed to Tokyo Shibaura

Electric Co., Ltd. In 1939, it merged with Tokyo Electric Co., and again with Toshiba Corporation in 1978. Toshiba developed and introduced a litany of innovative new products in Japan and abroad. Some examples of those are:

- 1875: The first workshop-produced telephone apparatus

- 1894: First Japanese water wheel generator (60k VA)

- 1916: First electronic receiving tube in Japan

- 1930: First electric washing machine and refrigerator in Japan

- 1931: First vacuum cleaner

- 1936: First high-powered radio broadcasting system in Japan

- 1940: First fluorescent lamp in Japan

- 1941: World's largest electrostatic X-ray plant

- 1942: First radar system in Japan

- 1952: First television transmitting equipment in Japan

- 1954: First digital computer in Japan

- 1955: First electric rice cooker

- 1957: First transistor radio in Japan

- 1959: First television and microwave oven in Japan

- 1962: First synthetic diamond in Japan

- 1963: First nuclear turbine generator in Japan

- 1978: First Japanese word processor

- 1982: First magnetic resonance imaging (MRI) and perpendicular magnetic recording system

- 1986: First laptop personal computer

- 1992: First filmless X-ray imaging equipment

- 1992: World's first 16-megabit flash memory

There are many other developments, such as electrical power generation, land communication, satellite communications, radar systems, semiconductors, and medical systems, that are credited to Toshiba. For decades, Toshiba held a leading position in the electrical and electronics industries and was a leader in the Japanese business community.

In fact, Mr. Taizo Ishizaka, Toshiba's President and Chairman, also served as the Chairman of Japan's Federation of Economic Organizations (Keidanren), a comprehensive economic organization comprising 1,512 Japanese companies and 107 nationwide industrial associations representing all forty-seven prefectures (as of April 1, 2023).

With those promised advantages of leading engineering achievement and leadership in the Japanese and international business worlds, why did Toshiba not take advantage of its competitive position?

The following are the signs of failure resulting from an unfavorable course. Toshiba survives today with approximately 100,000 employees worldwide and gets support from the Japanese community, but there is a lingering concern about inefficient internal management. The employees at Toshiba are mostly good-natured and work together comfortably, but they have lost their spirit of competitiveness. Although many people challenge themselves to improve their capacities and achieve better results in engineering development, they are less concerned about competitiveness in the market. Often, superior quality products were manufactured by Toshiba, but they failed in terms of competition in the market. As a result, lower pricing became the priority regardless of the quality of the product. All this boils down to management issues.

The Failure of Toshiba

Toshiba had weaknesses in internal executive management. Every time Toshiba faced a severe problem, the company had to depend on the skills of external management for help, like with the introduction of Mr. Taizo Ishizaka and Mr. Toshio Doko.

The Communist Party in Japan focused on Toshiba as a symbol of anti-capitalism right after World War II, organizing a strong labor union within the company. Toshiba was almost bankrupted by a company-wide, long-term strike. Management could not negotiate effectively with the union to cease the company-wide strike. The Japanese government and industrial leaders were very much concerned about Toshiba's situation, which led to discussions among its major shareholders (mostly insurance companies and banks). They elected Mr. Taizo Ishizaka, retired President of Dai-ichi Mutual Life Insurance Co., to restore Toshiba. Mr. Ishizaka became Executive Director of Tokyo Shibaura Electric Co., Ltd. in 1948 and assumed the role of President of Toshiba on April 1, 1949. He made a four-step plan to pursue the restoration of the company, as follows:

1. Downsize employees.

2. Restructure headquarters and dismiss some executives.

3. Enact financial planning.

4. Coordinate with International General

Electric Co., which was the major Toshiba shareholder.

Mr. Ishizaka successfully reduced the number of employees by 6,000 in one month. The company-wide strike was over through his dexterous negotiation with the union. Toshiba was subsequently restored after executing his four-step plan. Mr. Ishizaka became Chairman of the Japan Federation of Economic Organizations in 1956 because of his successful accomplishments at Toshiba. He then became the Chairman of Tokyo Shibaura Electric Co., Ltd. in 1957.

Toshiba began to lose discipline in its internal management again several years after Mr. Ishizaka's successor took the position of

President. The company's atmosphere became sumptuous from the top down because of rapid business growth, which led to a lack of discipline.

Toshio Doko, retired President of Ishikawajima-Harima Industries, Co., Ltd., was called in by Mr. Ishizaka to once again restore Toshiba by nominating him as the President of Tokyo Shibaura Electric Co., Ltd. in 1965. Mr. Doko realized that he had to reawaken Toshiba's executives and employees to the urgency of his reform. At the time, there was a bathroom and a kitchen with a professional chef in the President's room. Mr. Doko removed all these amenities. One large room was provided for all executives to share as their office space. Mr. Doko got to his office at 8:00 a.m. each morning, so other executives could not ignore being on time. He did this to change the culture of tardiness among executives.

Mr. Doko visited all Toshiba facilities to observe what they were doing. He also visited the office of the labor union to discuss issues directly, rather than asking union leaders to come to the President's office for negotiations. He told union members that he would not look at factory employees as laborers but as human beings. As a result, the working atmosphere changed. Mr. Doko became the Chairman of Tokyo Shibaura Electric Co., Ltd. in 1972.

Kiyoshi Hamada took a job at the Lamp & Tube Division of Tokyo Shibaura Electric Company, Ltd., right after he graduated from Keio University in 1957. The same year, Mr. Ishizaka became the Chairman of Toshiba. Kiyoshi observed that middle management was often disappointed with senior management's decision-making and felt discouraged from pursuing their own ideas. Instead of challenging senior management, they just griped.

Kiyoshi decided to approach a Senior Executive who oversaw the Lamp & Tube Division. He recognized the Executive's name from his graduation report at Keio University. His published book on mass-production management of lamp manufacturing at Toshiba motivated Kiyoshi to join the company and pursue his interest in production management as a profession. There was no way for Kiyoshi to approach the Executive's office through the normal channels because he was in such a high position at the company. As the only young newcomer, he decided to approach the Senior Executive at home by phone. The Executive listened as Kiyoshi introduced himself and explained the purpose of his call. He then invited Kiyoshi to his house that evening and listened to his concerns. Kiyoshi visited the Executive's house several more times, discussing management issues without specifying any names. He later noticed some improvements in management practices within the Lamp & Tube Division, though nobody knew why.

One day, the Executive of the Lamp & Tube Division asked Kiyoshi to accompany him to the headquarters building in Tokyo to visit Senior Executives. The Division Executive approached them in a large meeting room to request assistance with obtaining an import quota from the Japanese government for high-intensity fire bricks, which were used in the furnace to produce Braun tubes. Kiyoshi observed that no one in the room paid attention to his request for help.

Toshiba's consumer products were eventually consigned to manufacturers in China and other Asian countries, following the closure of its own manufacturing facilities in Japan, the US, Mexico, and other countries. Toshiba was no longer a manufacturer of consumer products, regardless of its superior engineering advantage.

Mr. Ishizaka, the Chairman of Toshiba, visited the company's New York office quite often during his business trips. He was one of the few top executives at Toshiba who spoke veritably fluent conversational English. His visits with the CEO of International General Electric Co. were natural and fluid, as he carried the conversation while maintaining his own pace in speaking English.

When Kiyoshi accompanied Mr. Ishizaka, he told Kiyoshi about the Executive Board meeting at Toshiba Headquarters. He complained that there was neither an argument nor further discussions raised by anyone responding to his request in the meeting. They obviously did not want to undergo any extreme change that might disturb their comfort.

Most of the executives who visited the US had to depend on interpreters to have business meetings with their clients because of their inability to communicate in English. The majority of their visits with clients were merely courtesy visits. They could not wait to finish their meetings and were more interested in going out for entertainment and shopping for their colleagues and families.

The top management of Toshiba was unaware of the seriousness of the political problem caused by Toshiba Machine (a subsidiary of Toshiba), which violated the Coordinating Committee for Multilateral Export Controls (COCOM) by exporting a precision milling machine to the Soviet Union. The precision milling machine was capable of manufacturing ultra-quiet screw shafts for submarines that rendered operating sounds nearly undetectable by sonar. Investigations by the US government and Congress, along with boycotts of Toshiba products, were intensifying. Toshiba America Inc. (TAI) did not conduct any business with Toshiba Machine, but protesters targeted TAI because of the Toshiba name. TAI lobbied the US government and Congress, explaining that TAI had not done any business with Toshiba Machine, and TAI employees wrote letters to members of Congress explaining the same. People continued boycotting campaigns toward Toshiba products for months.

Toshiba announced a picture-perfect set of in-house rules and regulations in compliance with various governmental standards that emphasized governance at all levels of the company. These were praised by business communities in Japan. The implementation of these rules and regulations, however, was not followed by Toshiba executives, and not all levels of management put them into practice.

Price competition in the US consumer market left TAI heavily in debt. Toshiba Corp. rescued TAI by strategically maneuvering to increase/decrease TAI's capital to clear its debts.

The top executives emphasized the company's financial status by fabricating accounting reports presented to the public. A typical example was the inflation of Toshiba's laptop computer business, portraying it as if it were profitable.

Failure to manage the Westinghouse Nuclear business in the United States almost brought Toshiba Corp. to bankruptcy. After acquiring Westinghouse, Toshiba appointed a new Chairman from among its executives. He later claimed that he had not received reports about the situation from management until the problem had already surfaced to the public. It was obvious he had not been involved with internal management at Westinghouse.

Toshiba was forced to give up two profitable business divisions, NAND-type Semiconductor and Medical Equipment, selling them to other companies to raise funds to cover the debts generated by the Westinghouse. Furthermore, Toshiba accepted investments from overseas activists to increase its funds. These activists then demanded concessions from Toshiba's management, causing further turmoil. Eventually, a group of Japanese companies raised funds and secured a bank loan, which resulted in a successful TOB (takeover bid) on the Tokyo Stock Exchange, allowing Toshiba to convert into a private entity. Toshiba Corp. was delisted from the Tokyo Stock Exchange on December 20, 2023, ending seventy-four years of membership.

Part II

CHAPTER 2
The Tenganji Temple

Kiyoshi Hamada was born in January 1935 at Tenganji Temple, the youngest of four children in the Hamada Family.

Tenganji Temple was built in 1678 as a family temple of the Matsudaira clan. It was one of three families from the Tokugawa dynasty, which governed Japan for over 250 years until it was defeated in the civil war in 1868. The temple was renovated in 1923, and the family crest of the hollyhock was displayed on the wooden door of the main hall, identifying the Tokugawa clan. The temple property was much larger in the Edo era, occupying an entire block, according to a display map at the Edo Museum in Ryogoku, Tokyo.

Main building of Tenganji Temple

The temple property was rich in nature, with fruit trees such as persimmon, pomegranate, summer orange, fig, and even banana. There were a lot of insects, birds, reptiles, and fish in two ponds, as well as hemp palms and bamboo fields, pre-World War II, before the renovation that took place in recent years. The Aizome River runs in front of the temple, surrounded by nature, with bush warblers flying and twittering everywhere.

The newly formed Government enacted the democratic system based on the independence of the three powers by the Constitution of the Empire of Japan in 1889, and Tenganji Temple gradually subdivided its property to local businesses.

The Matsudaira family remained a major property owner in the Kansai region and Tokyo, and carried the social status of viscount, honored by the newly formed Japanese government. When World War II ended in 1945, the Matsudaira family lost its social status and much of its land ownership due to new laws put in place by the General Headquarters of the US Allied Forces. This situation led the Matsudaira family to consolidate their family graves under one tombstone in the temple cemetery in the

1950s due to financial difficulties. Empty spaces in the cemetery were then offered to the public for family graves.

The grave of Dazai Shundai is kept in Tenganji Temple. Dazai Shundai was a noted Confucian scholar during the middle Edo period (1680–1747). According to Para Books, "He served as a retainer to Matsudaira Iadanori, Lord of Izushi in the province of Tajima, present-day Hyogo Prefecture. He had taught Confucianism that embraced both the study of poetry and literature and attention to practical concerns of economic and political life." The Tokyo Metropolitan Government designated Tenganji Temple as an official historic site in 1924.

Doki Hamada converted from samurai status to a Zen priest after the Civil War. Upon completing his training to become a Zen priest, he became the Superior Priest at Tenganji Temple. Because of his earlier occupation as a samurai in Yamanashi, samurai swords in varied sizes and shapes were concealed in hidden spaces in the storage rooms around the temple.

The Japanese military confiscated a large bronze bell and water retainers to convert to weaponry during World War II.

The Rinzai-shu sector, unlike other Zen sectors, allows priests to get married and have families. Masamichi Hamada (Kiyoshi's father) was born in 1889 as the firstborn son of Doki Hamada. After being trained at the Myoshinji Temple (the Headquarters of Rinzai-shu) in Kyoto, he succeeded his father as the Superior Priest of Tenganji Temple. Two prospective priest trainees and two housekeepers who worked at the temple lived in separate quarters of the temple.

Rinzai-shu practices meditation in several ways. The daily routine in the temple would start with Kiyoshi's father's chanting in the morning as the Superior Priest. He would then dust the inner temple as well as sweep the courtyard and entrance. After that, he would preach a sermon to parishioners and prepare seasonal services. Chores included sweeping and weeding in the cemetery and performing funeral services when requested. Once a year, he went out as a begging priest wearing a black monk's robe and a tall straw hat, with a shakuhachi (bamboo flute) in hand and a beggar's bag over his shoulder. This was to practice humbling himself in search of enlightenment.

When air raids by US bombers intensified in Tokyo during World War II, an enormous number of people lost their homes. Thankfully, Tenganji Temple was unscathed from the destruction of the air raid. Kiyoshi's father offered to let some families shelter in the temple until they were able to find a place to live on their own. Some families stayed for many years in different parts of the temple property.

Masamichi Hamada retired as the Superior Priest of Tenganji Temple in 1968.

Front of Tenganji Temple gate

CHAPTER 3
Pre-World War II to
the Post-War Period

Preschool Life

The first constitution (The Constitution of the Empire of Japan) was issued in 1889, and the first parliamentary session began in 1890. Japan engaged in war with China in 1894, and the peace treaty between the two nations was signed in 1895. The Japan-Britain Alliance agreement was signed in 1902. Japan declared war against Russia in 1904, intending to stop Russia's aggressive advancement into the Far East. The Japanese Navy destroyed the Russian Baltic Fleet in the Sea of Japan. The fleet had the reputation of being the largest and strongest naval power in the world at that time.

The peace treaty between Japan and Russia was signed in 1905, mediated by the US President Theodore Roosevelt as the Portsmouth Agreement.

World War I began in 1914, and Japan declared war on Germany. The war ended in 1918. Japan declared the founding of the state of Manchukuo in Manchuria in 1932. The following year, Japan withdrew from the League of Nations.

Kiyoshi Hamada was born amid growing militarism in Japan. When Kiyoshi was about three years old, right after the National Mobilization Law was promulgated in 1938, his father was drafted into the Japanese military. He was sent to Northern China until 1940. When his father was released from military duty, Kiyoshi's mother took him and his brother to Kanazawa, where their father had returned from China. Kiyoshi had no recollection of his father's face, and he looked like a stranger to him since he had been so young when his father left home.

Kiyoshi's mother, Mineko, had to take care of not only the household duties but also the temple's operation while Kiyoshi's father was on military duty. When commemoration of ancestors or funeral services were requested, she depended on a neighborhood priest to perform these services in the temple. She also had to manage a variety of temple-related tasks, such as contracting stonecutters to prepare new tombstones for graves, renewing the tatami mats, finding a carpenter to fix parts of the temple, and hiring a gardener to maintain the temple property.

Kiyoshi's mother held several teaching certificates: tea ceremony, flower arrangement, and koto playing, and she trained Kiyoshi's sisters to master these practices. She was an education-minded mother who made sure her children not only studied but also became honor students in school. Kiyoshi's sisters and brother did not disappoint her, remaining honorary students throughout their primary school years.

The living environment was one of hardship: sitting and sleeping on the smooth but hard surface of the tatami mat floor, with only the hibachi and kotatsu to warm up their hands and feet in the winter, and just an uchiwa (handheld fan) cooling them in the summer. Six rooms at the rear of the temple were for families, two rooms in the front of the temple were for trainees and housekeepers, and one reception room was for consultation with visitors. The two large rooms were for visitors to dine in after the temple services, in addition to the Hondo (the main hall of the temple). The Hamada family slept in one room together, lining up five futons side by side. They were covered by a huge net to protect them from mosquitoes in the summer and comforted by a hibachi with burning charcoal for warmth in the winter. The futons were stored during the day, so the same room could serve as the living room. Kiyoshi's father, after being released from military duty, claimed the second floor as his own for sleeping and meditation.

Local transportation was limited to electric streetcars, and walking was common. Entertainment took place mostly at home—book reading, children's songs, koto music, karuta (playing cards), sugoroku (a backgammon-like board game), hanetsuki (a kind of badminton), and flying kites for the New Year. There was no reading of manga books, with the exception of one cartoon—a personified bear who wore a military uniform and gear. Unlike a typical childhood, Kiyoshi had no toys except for one fire engine, awarded to him as a healthy baby by the City of Tokyo. Radio broadcasting was mostly limited to news. Daily shopping was done in the neighboring stores for people who visited neighbors to take grocery orders. Peddlers went around town in the early morning, offering fresh fish, shellfish, natto (fermented soybeans), and tofu, which they carried on their shoulders.

Kiyoshi, the youngest, was left alone while his sisters and brother were at school and met with their friends afterward. Going to kindergarten was a big challenge for him. That was the first time he had been away from his mother. He had to walk alone over two miles to his kindergarten, which was operated by the Kaneiji Temple (a family temple of the Tokugawa clan). He was a sad boy in class, often thinking of going back home.

Kiyoshi's mother spent over a week in December cooking a variety of extra foods and mochitsuki (making rice cakes) in preparation for the family's relaxation over the New Year. She took seven days off from daily cooking.

In the summer, Kiyoshi's mother took the family to the Izu Peninsula, a resort area known for its hot springs along the seashore. She usually watched from the balcony of the Japanese inn, while Kiyoshi and his brother enjoyed playing on the seashore.

Kiyoshi's mother also took the family to Nagoya, her birthplace, where her own mother, brothers, and sisters lived. The overnight train trip from Tokyo to Nagoya took eight hours and spanned 250 miles on a limited express train driven by a coal-burning locomotive. The train accommodations did not include air conditioning in the summer, so windows needed to be opened to get fresh air. The Tokaido Railway wound through many hills and mountains, and passengers had to close the windows every time the train went through a tunnel; otherwise, the inside became filled with black soot from the burning coal. By the time they got to the train station in Nagoya, their faces and nostrils were covered with soot. Kiyoshi was always excited to travel by train, but he ended up with motion sickness by the time they arrived at their destination because the train shook, bounced, and swayed so much. Kiyoshi's grandmother always welcomed the Hamada family, and they took time to visit their mother's brothers and sisters and their families.

Militarism affected all aspects of everyday life, including education, organizing neighborhood circles, exercising defense measures, and wearing military uniforms. Kiyoshi's father did not talk about any of his experiences in the China War to his family, and he wanted to keep them away from militarism as much as possible. He did not declare anti-war views, but he tried to maintain a peaceful atmosphere in his family and fulfill his duties in the temple. Sometimes, he had to face a controversial situation with a neighbor or some temple visitors, but he always lectured them on Zen principles.

Primary School,
The Beginning of World War II,
and Middle School

World War II began when Germany invaded Poland in 1939. The military alliance treaty between Japan, Germany, and Italy was signed in 1940. Army General Hideki Tojo formed a cabinet and attacked Pearl Harbor in Hawaii in 1941, initiating the Pacific War as part of World War II. National mobilization was declared. Young healthy men in town and young trainees in the temple disappeared after being drafted into military duty. The housekeepers were called back by their families to help with farming.

Kiyoshi was enrolled in primary school in April 1941, amid the rising atmosphere of militarism in Japan. He was a shy student, almost unnoticeable in class. However, he was a curious boy at home, looking around for interesting objects in the house. He took the alarm clock and disassembled it to satisfy his curiosity. He gave some of its parts to the boys in his neighborhood.

When his parents found out what Kiyoshi did, they placed him in the dark main building of the temple for discipline.

As the war intensified, the military-controlled government ordered female students in middle schools to work at manufacturing plants to provide necessary labor. Kiyoshi's sisters were sent to a plant in Tokyo. His brother, a senior in primary school, underwent military training by professional soldiers. His mother's youngest brother was drafted and sent to Manchuria in Northern China. Kiyoshi's father's younger brother was not drafted because he worked as an inspector for the Japanese Ministry of Education.

Between 1941 and 1944, the Japanese Navy lost the Battle of Midway to the US Navy, withdrew from Guadalcanal Island, and lost a battle at Leyte. Tokyo fell within the range of air raids by the US Air Force. The primary school decided to evacuate fourth- through sixth-year classes to Iidate Village in Fukushima Prefecture to protect students from the air raids. Kiyoshi was in the fourth year, so he, his classmates, and teachers went from Tokyo to Fukushima in 1944. Iidate Village was known for its hot springs that were believed to cure some skin diseases. They stayed in the only inn in the village, sharing accommodations with people who had skin diseases. Food preparation for students was extremely limited, and it was obvious that the local villagers did not welcome them. A small amount of rice mixed with cubes of potato and the outer skin of watermelon was the main dish. Some parents, including Kiyoshi's parents, sent some snacks to their children. The schoolteachers kept all the snacks in their room, and students were allowed to eat them there. In the meantime, the teachers served the snacks to themselves instead of keeping them for the students. The teachers lost Kiyoshi's respect, as he felt they were taking advantage of their position instead of caring for the welfare of their students.

Within ten months, Kiyoshi developed an acute kidney disease caused by undernourishment. His mother came to Fukushima Hospital, where he was under medical treatment, and took him back to Tokyo. Kiyoshi found that the Japanese Military Police had occupied his school to use as their station base. There was no school left to attend.

The United States, England, and the Soviet Union held a meeting at Yalta. US B-29 bombers were sighted flying over Tokyo. Air raids by the US Air Force over Tokyo began intensifying, destroying civilian houses. The shrill sound of bombs falling from the sky, a fricative sound, made the Hamada family feel helpless. Kiyoshi's father provided shelter in the backyard of the temple. The shelter was so small and musty in the dark. It was just about big enough to accommodate six of the Hamada family members.

In April 1945, Kiyoshi's parents decided to evacuate their family (except for two daughters, who remained in the temple to work in the plants due to military mobilization orders) to the temple in Kofu in the Yamanashi Prefecture. Kiyoshi's brother enrolled in middle school, and Kiyoshi was in the fifth year of elementary school. The only practice in the class he remembered was memorizing the genealogy of Japanese emperors. He and his classmates were sent to farmers nearby to work in the rice fields. When they got out of the rice fields, they had to pull bloodsuckers from their legs. Kiyoshi and his classmates were also sent to farmers to peel the bark of mulberry trees by hand. They were told that the peeled bark would be used to make Army uniforms.

Kofu City was completely destroyed by a US air raid on the night of July 6, 1945. The Hamada family lived just on the outskirts of the city, but twenty-four incendiary bombs exploded in the air, shooting down everywhere. Kiyoshi had to knock away a burning detonator from a bomb flying through the air with his padded head protector on hand. The Hamada family ducked into the ditch of a rice field to avoid the flying pieces. There was fire all around them, and the city of Kofu burned like hell. Kiyoshi's father took Fumimasa and Kiyoshi to the city the next day. They saw the destruction of the city and charred, dead human bodies piled up in its central park.

Kiyoshi found numerous unexploded bombs in the rice fields around the temple area. The rice field was very soft, watery ground, so the bombs did not detonate upon landing. He pulled a bomb out from the rice fields and disengaged the detonator with a screwdriver. He then took out the oil gel contained in cotton gauze from the shell. He was curious to know what the bomb was made out of and played with the burning gel.

The Potsdam Conference was held in Potsdam by the United States, the United Kingdom, and the Soviet Union. President Harry S. Truman, Prime Minister Winston Churchill, and General Secretary Joseph Stalin represented their nations on July 26, 1945.

An atomic bomb exploded over Hiroshima on August 6, 1945. The Soviet Union declared war on Japan on August 8. A second atomic bomb exploded over Nagasaki on August 9. Japan accepted the Potsdam Declaration on August 14. Japanese Emperor Hirohito declared the end of the war on August 15, and Japan signed an instrument of unconditional surrender on September 2. The US government announced its Initial Post-Surrender Policy for Japan on September 22. On October 4, the US Military General Headquarters (GHQ), under General MacArthur, issued an order for democratization.

Kiyoshi's father took Kiyoshi and his brother to their relatives in the Nagoya area to avoid the uncertain situation in Tokyo right after the war. The Hamada family realized that staying for an extended length of time there was not welcomed by their relatives, so Kiyoshi's father decided to bring his family back to Tokyo in the spring of 1946.

Kiyoshi's first assignment in the sixth-year class was to block out unwanted lines in the textbooks, following instructions from the Japanese government in response to GHQ guidelines. His life in primary school was shaped almost entirely by World War II. He did not receive a decent education at school. It felt like a black hole of education.

The Constitution of Japan came into effect on May 3, 1947. As a result, the government organization, social structures, the education system, and people's behavior changed drastically.

In April 1947, Kiyoshi's parents decided to enroll Kiyoshi in a private middle school with the new education system, where his brother had been enrolled under the old system. Going through the hardships of not only limited food and clothing but also the fear of death in wartime, Kiyoshi's interests began to shift to the meaning of life rather than learning from textbooks in school. He had two close classmates interested in the same subject. They read many shishosetsu (novels based on the writer's own life experiences) and exchanged opinions about the meaning of life. Kiyoshi's observations on life came from living in the temple, where people came for ancestry worship and to visit the cemetery. The question that came to Kiyoshi was: What is living for, and what is life beyond death, if anything? The three boys exchanged opinions on the topic endlessly.

The food supply, rationed by the local government, was so limited that no family was able to survive solely on the rations. Farmers outside of Tokyo kept their food for themselves. The newspaper reported on a judge who tried to prove that he could not survive on the food rations alone. He died of starvation within a short time.

New currency denominations made it more difficult for people to obtain food from the underground market. Kiyoshi's mother and sisters carried their clothing to farmers outside of Tokyo to exchange them for vegetables and rice. The train was so congested that it was impossible to get in through the door. They had to climb in through the windows instead. His mother had a strong will to support her family and was determined to do so, no matter how difficult, dangerous, or even unlawful things became. Kiyoshi accompanied her once to get food supplies in exchange for the family's clothes from farmers outside of Tokyo. He got on the train through a window and carried back as much exchanged food as possible.

CHAPTER 4
Education Under Stressful Living Standards

The Korean War began on June 25, 1950. The San Francisco Peace Treaty, along with the Japan-US Security Treaty, was signed on September 8, 1951. Japan became a logistical base for the US military during the Korean War. The Japan-US Security Treaty improved Japan's position internationally. Domestic business began benefiting from the Korean War , serving as supply sources for the US military in Korea. However, the standard of living in Japan was still low.

Kiyoshi began to wonder how to advance to high school once he reached the third year of middle school. His parents expected him to advance to high school in the same Keika school system. When he asked them about other options, they had no other plan for him other than to continue in the same school system. His parents primarily focused on Kiyoshi's brother as the firstborn son in the family.

Kiyoshi's classmates were preparing to take an achievement test (like a proficiency test) that the government provided as an equal opportunity for students to advance to their desired high school. The trial achievement test did not make Kiyoshi comfortable. He would have preferred to express his own response to the subjects in writing rather than simply answering "yes" or "no." Kiyoshi discovered that he could apply to Keio High School (where his brother was already enrolled). Keio High School practiced traditional examination rather than the achievement test. Kiyoshi's parents were quite skeptical of him because of his mediocre grades in middle school. Competition for the entrance examination was exceptionally high at Keio High School. Kiyoshi's brother said that it was too late for Kiyoshi because he had not prepared for the examination for a reasonable length of time. When Kiyoshi insisted, his brother suggested that he study the textbooks from his middle school, so he did. He then applied for the entrance examination at Keio High School. Kiyoshi's parents did not expect him to pass the examination. Kiyoshi and his mother went to look for his name on the display board of accepted applicants at Keio High School. To their surprise, his name was on the board. Student life at Keio High School began on April 1, 1950.

Keio High School

Keio was established in 1858 by Yukichi Fukuzawa as the first private institution in Japan. The current Keio school system includes institutions from primary school through two kinds of middle schools and high schools, as well as universities for undergraduate, graduate, and doctorate degrees in various departments.

The Keio High School building was located in Hiyoshi, Kanagawa Prefecture, and was built before World War II. It was a heavy, three-story concrete building, one hundred meters long. A 400-meter Olympic-standard track and field and tennis courts were also part of the campus. The Japanese Navy used the building as its headquarters during World War II, and the US Navy used it for its temporary administrative operations. Commuting from Tenganji Temple to the high school took almost two and a half hours by electric streetcar, subway, and train (via the Toyoko line).

Keio High School had twenty classes per year, with fifty students in each class, meaning 1,000 students per year for a total of 3,000 male students. The Keio High School for Girls, with a smaller number of students, was in Tokyo.

There were many interesting students in Kiyoshi's class, some who advanced from Keio Middle Schools. Kiyoshi's parents provided him with a new black school uniform and a black hat, but they could not afford to buy a new pair of shoes, so his father gave him his own red-brown shoes.

Kiyoshi started to associate with a few close friends in class. Soon, his personal interests shifted to reading translated foreign literature, particularly European literature. One of his classmates' fathers was a popular fiction novelist. When he invited Kiyoshi to visit his house in Kamakura, Kiyoshi was amazed by the book collection in the father's library that spanned the wall from floor to ceiling all around the room. That collection became Kiyoshi's source of book reading. The books he selected were mostly about internal struggles in personal behavior, individuality, and existentialism, which analyzed human behavior when placed in extreme circumstances. But there was no answer to what life was about. Is death the end of life? Individualism and the meaning of life were Kiyoshi's focus. Studying at school was not the goal of life. It was necessary for him to understand the goal of life, which would be realized later.

Some other classmates exposed Kiyoshi to new experiences. He received invitations to attend the theater, classical music concerts, sumo wrestling events, fireworks at the Sumida River, mountain climbing, skiing, playing tennis, and so on.

During his third year of high school, Kiyoshi turned his attention to studying everything in class. All his test results were nearly perfect. The homeroom teacher was not satisfied when his test result was eighty instead of one hundred. Kiyoshi's mother was surprised to hear only favorable comments about Kiyoshi from his homeroom teacher when she attended parent meetings.

Kiyoshi's possible choices were economics, literature, law school, medical school, or engineering when advancing to Keio University. His parents were still struggling financially to support their children. The economic boom from the Korean War did not have any positive effects on the temple. Kiyoshi's mother wanted him to become a medical doctor, but that required a longer financial dependence on his parents, and it was not his first choice anyway. So, Kiyoshi enrolled in the Economics Department at Keio University.

Keio University

The Japanese Self-Defense Forces were established on June 9, 1954. The United Nations General Assembly unanimously voted to accept Japan as a member on December 18, 1956. Although Japan began to be recognized by the international community, the domestic standard of living remained low under strict government economic control.

Kiyoshi's college life began in the Economics Department on April 1, 1953. The first two years of study at Keio University were in Hiyoshi, Kanagawa Prefecture. Kiyoshi's parents took on the burden of his tuition, textbooks, transportation, and pocket money.

The Economics Department consisted of thirteen classes with fifty students per class. The total number of students in the department was about 650 per year, for a total of 2,600. About half of Kiyoshi's classmates were not Keio High School graduates. They came from other high schools after going through a highly competitive entrance examination by Keio University. It was in the same location as Keio High School, where he graduated, but the college buildings were separated from the high school building. Classrooms were in a semi-cylindrical roof structure, originally built for temporary use by the US Navy Administration office after World War II. The experience in his last year of Keio High School gave Kiyoshi some confidence that he could achieve satisfactory results if he put effort into his studies.

Kiyoshi extended his coursework into different departments to fulfill his desire to acquire innumerable knowledge, rather than limiting himself to the Economics Department. He became interested in fulfilling his curiosity about a variety of subjects and was not concerned about getting good grades in the Economics Department. A class in Music Appreciation in the Literature Department gave him insight into listening to classical music. Another class in Living English in the Literature Department sparked Kiyoshi's interest in learning English. The Professor of this subject introduced real English from a variety of literature, which he called "Living English." The language was not necessarily bound by grammar. The way English people used it was considered the real English language, so the class needed to understand and use it that way. The professor lived in England during his boyhood because his father was a Japanese Diplomat to the United Kingdom. He quoted many examples from English Literature and asked the class to exercise Living English. Kiyoshi also took courses in Teaching Practice of English and Sociology in the Literature Department.

His general education for the first two years of college gave Kiyoshi the opportunity to fulfill his interests and obtain a variety of knowledge, rather than limiting him to taking courses only in the Economics Department. He still had an unanswered question in his mind regarding what life was about. Observing Zen practice in the temple, facing the cemetery at the backyard of the temple, attending philosophy and psychology classes in college, and reading books that analyzed human behavior did not give him a clear answer about the relationship between body and soul. The end of the body by death was understandable, but where does the soul go to exist? Many religions mentioned heavenly life, but nobody had experienced the reality of its existence—only believed, fantasized, or simply put trust in God. What would the achievements in his life mean?

Kiyoshi joined the Denen Tennis Club in the town of Denenchofu and had a fun time swimming in Hamanako (Lake Hamana) with his friend during the summer of his first two years of college. He also had a group of friends, five classmates, with whom he walked on the peaks of mountains for a week or two each summer.

The location of the third and fourth years of college changed to Mita, Tokyo, from Hiyoshi, Kanagawa Prefecture. These years were more focused on the selected subject of study. After scrutinizing the possibilities of what direction to take, Kiyoshi decided to pursue Business Administration rather than continue studying the Theory of Economics. The main purpose of studying in the undergraduate college in the

Economics Department was to learn, analyze, and understand the theory of economics. Kiyoshi applied to the seminar group under Professor Dr. Yasuo Kotaka, who oversaw Business Administration.

About thirty students began assembling under Professor Kotaka and proceeded to study and discuss subjects in which they were interested. As the seminar's session progressed, a few students in the group became very close friends of Kiyoshi, exchanging opinions outside of class. Kiyoshi began not only studying established theories from books but also became interested in developing his own thoughts. He also formed a friendship with Mr. Kojima, an Assistant to Professor Kotaka, exchanging all kinds of ideas not related to any subject in the seminar. This friendship helped Kiyoshi to fulfill his mental musings on human life issues. Their conversations gave Kiyoshi some comfort that he was not the only one curious about the subject.

Three students, including Kiyoshi, were selected to represent Keio University at the annual meeting of the Learned Society of All

Japan Collegian Accounting, held at Kansei Gakuin University in Nishinomiya, Hyogo Prefecture. Soichi Kaneko presented his report at the meeting.

The intense study of Kotaka's seminar minimized Kiyoshi's attention to his other subjects in the Economics Department. He began focusing on developing a mathematical formula to establish direct/indirect costs to the product life cycle. A computer system was not available at Keio University, so Kiyoshi could not prove his theory by handling mass data through a computer. His work remained as an unfinished theory. This work would not typically be considered an undergraduate study, but Professor Kotaka did not object; rather, he encouraged Kiyoshi to continue his own studies. His third year was a very fruitful one, during which he developed all aspects of his interests. His intense studying led to a lack of athletic activity, resulting in the loss of some physical strength. Soichi Kaneko, one of his best friends in the seminar, invited him to go skiing in the mountains and to participate in other outdoor activities.

Kiyoshi had to decide what his future life would hold, and Professor Kotaka suggested that he advance to graduate courses. There were a few things he had to consider—his parents' financial burden for him to stay longer in college (his brother was already in the graduate course in economics), his desire to be independent from his parents, and his goal of applying his studied theory of production management in the real world. While he was working on his graduation report during his fourth year, he found a book in the library of Keio University. The book introduced mass-production management at Toshiba, which was a real application of mass-production management rather than a written theory. That book helped him understand factual issues in mass-production management. Kiyoshi's interest in applying his work to the real world, such as at Toshiba, grew from there.

Keio University issued two recommendation letters to each student for job applications to corporations/other organizations.

Business activity had begun to progress in Japan, but it was not enough for business firms to employ all new college graduate applicants. The success rate of getting a job was relatively low. Kiyoshi applied for a job at Toshiba as his first choice and applied to another company as his second choice. Most corporations set the entrance examination for the same day, so if an applicant failed his or her first choice, the next examination would be available only for the least desirable organizations.

Toshiba gave a written test to all applicants, and for those who passed it, the next step was an interview with corporate executives as the final selection. An applicant was called into a large conference room, alone, facing the Headquarters and Division Executives , who posed many questions. When Kiyoshi was called into the conference room, he did not know what kind of questions he would have to respond to. He only remembered one question that the Human Resources Executive asked him, which was: "What would you do if Japan had to engage in war again? Would you join in a war for the nation of Japan?" Kiyoshi thought quickly in his mind for an answer, then replied, "I do not wish to answer to this hypothetical question. When the time comes, I will decide considering all related circumstances."

The Korean War was over, and the possibility of war in Vietnam was underway. Kiyoshi thought about his third choice in case he did not get a job. He chose the National Broadcasting Association (NHK), which did not require applicants to submit a letter of recommendation from college and used the achievement test. He was always bothered that he avoided the achievement test while applying for high school, and wanted to challenge his ability to overcome it. Three thousand applicants applied for fewer than fifty jobs at NHK. Kiyoshi's strategy was simple. He was going to mark "yes" or "no" for questions he was sure of and went back to take more time to consider unanswered questions.

A letter from Toshiba informed Kiyoshi of the acceptance of his job application. When he received a telephone call from NHK for an interview, he knew this meant he had passed the written test. He was happy to decline the job interview at NHK, having proved his ability to overcome the achievement test.

As the end of his fourth year in college approached, preparation for the graduation examination occupied most of his time. Kiyoshi was concerned about whether he had covered all the required courses to graduate from the Economics Department. Keio University did not provide a counseling service to help with students' concerns. Soichi's father invited six of Soichi's friends to visit his company's facilities in Kyushu. Kiyoshi was one of them. They spent two weeks on a trip to Kyushu and went directly to the graduation ceremony at Keio University from there. Kiyoshi hoped that he and all his friends would receive a diploma. They were happy to receive their diplomas on March 31, 1957, from the Economics Department of Keio University.

Part III

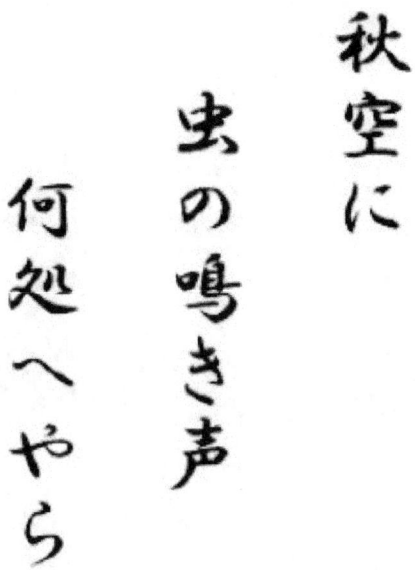

In the autumn sky

the sound of an insect

where did it go

The sound of an insect disappeared somewhere
in the autumn sky.

CHAPTER 5
Getting Started Working at Toshiba

One hundred eleven new college graduate employees gathered in a large hall at Toshiba's Headquarters building for their entrance ceremony in Tokyo on April 1, 1957. All attendees were then guided to the Toshiba school in Kawasaki, Kanagawa Prefecture, for orientation and were told they would work at six manufacturing plants and laboratories for three months before receiving a formal job assignment. The company provided a facility, like a dormitory, for all new college graduate employees to stay together in Kawasaki. Kiyoshi was assigned to work at four manufacturing plants and two laboratories, and he shared a room with two other colleagues. The experience at plants manufacturing radio receivers, home appliances, communication equipment, and heavy industrial products—as well as at two laboratories—was valuable to Kiyoshi, acquainting him with Toshiba's manufacturing operations. The job assignments were announced to all new college graduate employees at the end of three months. Kiyoshi was assigned to the Manufacturing Management Department in the Lamp & Tube Division, which was his first choice for an assignment.

CHAPTER 6
Unusual Assignments
at Toshiba

When Kiyoshi reported to his section in the department in Kawasaki, a new set of brand-new desk and chair were provided to him He was introduced to his colleagues and oriented to his job assignment.

There were many raw materials needed for manufacturing products as well as for engineering research. Some materials had to be imported from abroad because those items were not available in Japan. The Japanese government tightly controlled the import business due to limited foreign currency reserves. It was almost impossible for an individual company to obtain an import permit from the Ministry of International Trade and Industry (MITI). The Electronic Industries Association of Japan (EIAJ) represented member companies in negotiations with MITI to secure import quotas for necessary items. Toshiba held the Chairmanship at EIAJ. Kiyoshi, just a freshman beginning to work, was assigned to prepare the necessary data for items that the Lamp & Tube Division needed to import. He attended a meeting at EIAJ, not only submitting his list from Toshiba but also compiling all items from other member companies.

Kiyoshi never expected to be doing this kind of work in the Production Management Department, but department management did not see a place in routine work for him there. He was still looking for an opportunity to get involved in the core work of the department. General Electric Co. (GE) had been a major shareholder of Toshiba since pre-World War II, and the Lamp & Tube Division had implemented GE's production management method since then. Kiyoshi found the original

GE document in the archive files in the Division. He started reading the documents in his spare time, looking for something related to cost control theory. Unfortunately, his free time was dwindling. He had to prepare graphs outlining the prospects of color television in the domestic market to persuade MITI to issue import permits for the requested electronics. Materials included high-heat-resistant bricks to produce the Braun tubes for color televisions and germanium for transistors. Kiyoshi coordinated with other representatives from member electronics companies, consolidating all requests with his supporting data documents and submitting them as the industry's collective import quota request to the Deputy Manager of the Electronics Industry Section in MITI.

Since Toshiba was the leading manufacturer of semiconductors, the Deputy Manager of the Electronic Industry Section of MITI asked Kiyoshi to provide an explanatory document on semiconductors in plain language. Kiyoshi consulted with semiconductor engineers at Toshiba, wrote a document in his own words, and submitted it to him. The Deputy Manager told Kiyoshi that his document on semiconductors would be included in MITI's yearbook. The Deputy Manager, decades after he left MITI, was elected Governor of Oita Prefecture in Kyushu.

The abacus was the common tool used to handle figures when Kiyoshi began working at Toshiba. The company had a mainframe computer from GE for use in engineering design. It began to explore the introduction of a computer system for business administration. Top management requested that all divisions and specific departments at Headquarters select personnel to study how to introduce a computer system to the company. The Operations Research Group (OR Group) was then set up. Kiyoshi was nominated to join the OR Group, representing the Lamp & Tube Division. The activity of the OR Group was held outside of normal working hours. This group of approximately ten people began discussing how to proceed with their study. The group leader presented a document on the logistics system practiced by the US military. The group concluded, after studying the logistics system for a few weeks, that their first inevitable work was to establish a company-wide standardized coding system. The OR Group approached the top executives, recommending the plan. Letters from the President were sent to all executives in the company, requesting their cooperation with the OR Group to establish the new company-wide uniform coding system. Most divisions had their own coding systems for accounting, products, components, and materials, but these were not standardized across divisions in the company.

As Toshiba recognized a growing opportunity to export electron tubes and semiconductors, the Foreign Trade Division decided to form a new section dedicated to the exportation of lamps, electronic tubes, and semiconductors. In response, the Lamp & Tube Division decided to send a group of people to operate this new section in the Foreign Trade Division. The elected manager of the Production Management Department selected his group to be transferred to the Foreign Trade Division. Kiyoshi was one of five chosen. This was the end of his aspiration to be involved in production management and to implement his ideas for cost accounting in the future.

The Foreign Trade Division

Kiyoshi reported to the Foreign Trade Division in the Mitsui Building in Tokyo on April 1, 1960. The four other transferees from the Lamp & Tube Division were there, joined by five other members from the Foreign Trade Division to this Third Export Section. Mr. Takanobu Yoshihara, as a section manager from the Lamp & Tube Division, led the new ten-person section. Kiyoshi was assigned to oversee business planning and administration. Since Toshiba was acknowledged as an engineering enterprise in the international business community, constant inquiries about business opportunities from abroad overwhelmed the Third Export Section. Inquiries about electron tubes and semiconductors needed engineering negotiations in order to meet future customers' specifications. Kiyoshi gathered all business prospects and actual results of business transactions from section members and reported the weekly and monthly business activity to Division Management. He was responsible for developing business plans and preparing written business contracts when negotiations reached an agreement. He often consulted the International Division to furnish documents for formal business agreements.

The Division Management asked Kiyoshi to research prospective markets in South American countries. He spent time visiting the library of the US Embassy and other libraries to obtain economic data and related information. He submitted his concluding report on prospective business in South America to Division Management.

The United States and Canada separately began investigations into Toshiba's business involving components of receiving tubes imported to the US and Canada, respectively, under the Anti-Dumping Act. These actions were taken based on claims made by certain domestic business entities. The Third Export Section was in charge of those businesses exporting components of receiving tubes to major electronic companies like RCA, Motorola, Raytheon, Canadian Marconi, and others. Kiyoshi was assigned to provide counterevidence for all related components of receiving tubes exported to these companies from the beginning to the present day. He developed matrix lists of all components for every model number of receiving tubes. The Cost Accounting Department coordinated with Kiyoshi to purvey the cost data for every component of the targeted receiving tubes. It took him about four months to furnish two different handwritten lists of matrices covering all related components of receiving tubes targeted by the United States and Canada, respectively. Letters were typed refuting the unfair claim of the Anti-Dumping Act against Toshiba products. Kiyoshi delivered each set of documents to the US Embassy and the Canadian Embassy. Both governments dismissed the cases a few years later, due to unambiguous evidence refuting the claims of dumping practices by Toshiba.

Kiyoshi was enrolled in the Japan-US English Conversation School for six months, requested by the Human Resources Department, while he was in the midst of working to prepare data for the Anti-Dumping case. He returned to his office to continue working on the case after class, which was over at 3 p.m. every day. He went home at midnight every weekday and worked on the weekends. It was impossible for Kiyoshi to have time to complete homework for class the next day. Most of his classmates were from business entities that had internal selection processes to qualify for enrollment in the school. This was the first time that Toshiba had sent three employees to the school without an internal selection process.

Three months into the class at the Japan-US English Conversation School, Kiyoshi was free from the work of the Anti-Dumping Act cases. He decided to obtain a driver's license after class, going to Harumi Driving School to apply for the written test and driving tests. He received a phone call at Harumi from Mr. Takamiya, the Manager of Human Resources at Toshiba Headquarters. Mr. Takamiya demanded that Kiyoshi report to his office ASAP. It was Kiyoshi's own free time after the class, but Mr. Takamiya insisted that Kiyoshi report to his office anyway. Mr. Takamiya told Kiyoshi upon arrival at his office that an entrance examination for the Business School of Harvard University would be available the next day. He commanded Kiyoshi to apply for the examination. Kiyoshi resisted, stating that he was not qualified or capable of applying for that kind of test, and there were more suitable people in Toshiba than Kiyoshi. He also did not have enough time to prepare the necessary paperwork required to submit for the test. Mr. Takamiya told Kiyoshi that he was not concerned about the result of the examination, but Kiyoshi should just try it. Under the circumstances, Kiyoshi could not refuse, though he felt he was being used like a guinea pig. He spent the whole night, unmotivated, preparing the paperwork to apply for the test at Harvard Business School. When he arrived at the designated location for the test, a large university auditorium, 1,500 applicants were waiting there. Another location in Osaka was conducting the same test for another 1,500 applicants at the same time. A professor from Harvard University read an editorial article on international issues from *The New York Times*, then asked applicants to summarize it and state their own opinions within thirty minutes. It was too hard for Kiyoshi to comprehend the content, and he could not, therefore, express his opinion properly. He was told that only three out of 3,000 applicants would be accepted into the Business School. Most of the applicants spent years preparing for the examination. Kiyoshi went back to Mr. Takamiya's office immediately after the test and told him that he should never direct any employees without ample preparation to apply this kind of test in the future. Kiyoshi received his driver's license from the City of Tokyo. His normal routine work began in the office.

Business opportunities expanded rapidly, but domestic financial resources were limited for Toshiba, making it difficult to increase its investment in manufacturing facilities. The domestic inflation rate was high, pushing interest rates to 20 percent. In the meantime, the United States began experiencing a recession, with interest rates at 7 percent. Toshiba decided to raise funds by issuing American Depositary Receipts (ADRs) in the US financial market, taking advantage of the difference in interest rates between the two countries. Toshiba quickly realized, after issuing ADRs, the necessity of responding to numerous inquiries about the company from ADR owners in the United States, so the company planned to open an official Toshiba office in the US.. Mr. Yoshihara and Kiyoshi were selected to open the first Toshiba office in the United States, located in Manhattan, New York City. They had only three months to prepare for their departure to the United States. It was the beginning of 1962, and Kyoshi had worked for the Foreign Trade Division for less than two years.

Every assignment given to Kiyoshi was a new challenge. He did not have enough of a learning curve. He had to take every task as a test of his ability to manage and accomplish the desired results on time. There was not ample time to complain because the decision had already been made before he was directed to work on his new job assignment.

Mr. Yoshihara and Kiyoshi visited the main manufacturing plant of the Lamp & Tube Division in Himeji, Hyogo Prefecture. Kiyoshi began preparing his personal belongings to be shipped by boat. Toshiba prepared his Japanese passport, US visa, and other necessary legal documents, in addition to $197.55 in cash, $1,340.00 in traveler's checks, a one-way airline ticket to New York, and hotel reservations for stopovers. He did not have any time to say goodbye to his friends.

Toshiba's First Official Office in the United States

Kiyoshi's parents gathered family members and relatives at Tenganji Temple for a farewell dinner party for Kiyoshi. There were many people seeing off Mr. Yoshihara, accompanied by his family, and Kiyoshi at Haneda Airport on April 7, 1962: family members, friends, and colleagues from the Foreign Trade Division. PanAm Airlines took them to Honolulu, Hawaii, for an overnight stay, and then to San Francisco, California, for a two-night stay. Then, they finally arrived at Idlewild International Airport in New York on April 10, 1962. It was Kiyoshi's first air travel. He had no prior knowledge of New York City until he landed. He did not even realize that Manhattan was an island between the Hudson and East Rivers. But being a city boy in Tokyo, this city environment was not unfamiliar to Kiyoshi.

A Toshiba liaison and a few people from Mitsui & Co. took Mr. Yoshihara, his family, and Kiyoshi to the Hotel Mayflower on 97th Street and West End Avenue in Manhattan, where they stayed for a month. Toshiba's first official office was a one-room office rented from Mitsui & Co. at 530 Fifth Avenue in New York City.

Mr. Yoshihara and Kiyoshi began looking for an apartment to live in. Most Japanese businesspeople were living in Queens, NY, close to Idlewild International Airport, which was convenient for hosting visitors from Japan. Mr. Yoshihara and Kiyoshi searched for an apartment in northern New York City for a more reasonable living environment, as advised by some people they knew. The Riverdale area came to their attention, and they found apartments there. Mr. Yoshihara wanted Kiyoshi to live in the same apartment building because he was limited in his English communication ability. Kiyoshi took a studio apartment on the seventh floor overlooking a private residential area and the Hudson River.

Mr. Sakamaki, Soichi's brother-in-law, who was working at Daiichi Bank (USA), helped Kiyoshi with purchasing rugs, furniture, utensils, tableware, and a used car. Kiyoshi had to manage a monthly spending allowance of $500.00, which was Toshiba's monthly net pay in New York. In the meantime, Kiyoshi obtained a New York State driver's license. With that, they were ready to begin work in the new office.

The official purpose of the liaison office was to serve ADR holders in the United States.

The actual commission, however, was to promote Toshiba's business as a liaison and to do market research for the company's business practices in the United States. A telex machine in the office printed all kinds of requests from Toshiba Headquarters and Division Management every day. Mr. Yoshihara checked 10 to 20-foot-long rolls of printed telex paper first thing in the morning and discussed with Kiyoshi who was going to handle each request. Some requests were handled by phone calls to Toshiba's customers to obtain the information needed and then send the reply to the requester in Japan by telex by the day's end. Another task was to make appointments with Toshiba's customers to visit specified locations all over the country. This could mean traveling by car or by air. Many visitors from Toshiba asked Kiyoshi to accompany them when visiting their contacts in the United States. Some visitors were engineers discussing engineering issues with Toshiba's customers to promote more business opportunities. The department managers from the Foreign Trade Division requested that Kiyoshi accompany them to visit Toshiba's customers for business negotiations. Kiyoshi heard the news on the radio that President John F. Kennedy had been assassinated as he was driving back to the office from the US Testing Co. in New Jersey on November 22, 1963.

The World's Fair in Flushing Meadows, New York, the International Trade Fair at McCormick Place in Chicago, and the International Trade Fair in Dallas, Texas, were events where Kiyoshi displayed Toshiba products just for demonstration purposes.

The first portable transistor television set was soon developed by Toshiba. An engineer who developed this transistor TV set came to New York for the purpose of testing the reception capabilities of TV broadcasts in fringe areas across the United States. Kiyoshi accompanied the engineer in the different areas of New York and the West Coast. After arriving in Los Angeles, the engineer, Kiyoshi, and his business associates drove overnight to San Francisco via Fresno for a reception test.

Toshiba executives frequently sojourned at the New York office, requesting Mr. Yoshihara or Kiyoshi accompany them for courtesy visits to GE, a major shareholder of Toshiba, and to visit some critical Toshiba customers. They escorted the executives for fun on the weekends, too. It was seven days a week and 24 hours a day of paying attention to their visitors. Kiyoshi's physical condition was not ideal for this kind of highly demanding work. His stamina was low, and he was always concerned about getting motion sickness on the plane due to his dropped stomach. There was no other person to take his job, and he could not ignore the requirements from Tokyo. He had to endure the task of getting the job done.

Kiyoshi was invited by Mr. and Mrs. Sakamaki for dinner at their apartment. Mrs. Sakamaki (Soichi's sister) prepared a sukiyaki dinner, which was so delicious, and provided a warm reception that eased Kiyoshi's mental tension. Soichi stayed at Kiyoshi's apartment for a while after he finished attending Purdue University. When Kiyoshi had free time on weekends, they went out to practice golf at City Island. This, too, relieved some of Kiyoshi's tension.

Toshiba depended on exporters, importers, and distributors to market Toshiba brand products in the US market. The Toshiba New York office did not have the legal status to do business in the United States. A plan to establish a corporation to do business in the United States became the main task for the New York office.

Toshiba America Inc. (TAI) was incorporated on April 1, 1965, in the State of Delaware. The staff from Toshiba increased to ten people: President, Treasurer, marketing planning, sales and marketing, and several engineers. TAI assigned Kiyoshi to conduct market research and lay the groundwork for sales activities.

The Foreign Trade Division wanted to continue doing business with exporters/importers and distributors for the high-volume business of color televisions. TAI urged the management of the Foreign Trade Division to allow it to market the Toshiba brand color televisions in the United States and have the Foreign Trade Division concentrate on the business of Original Equipment Manufacturer (OEM) under its private brand. Kiyoshi discouraged importers and distributors from doing business with TAI. It was a big task for TAI to establish its own sales and marketing network, but if the company missed the opportunity to manage its own sales/marketing activity of Toshiba brand products in the United States, Toshiba would be making the same mistake as the transistor radio business—being dragged into a pricing competition.

The Foreign Trade Division finally gave in to TAI, allowing it to take responsibility for handling the sales and marketing of Toshiba brand products, including color televisions, in the US market.

The time came for Kiyoshi to return to the Foreign Trade Division in Tokyo after working for three and a half years in New York. He had grown increasingly frustrated with the top executives' mishandling of decision-making and their behavior. Many capable engineers were frustrated with being caught between prospective customers and poor decisions made by Toshiba Headquarters. Most executives who visited TAI made only courtesy calls to Toshiba's clients in the United States due to their limited proficiency in English and instead looked out for their personal interests, like shopping and entertainment. Some of Kiyoshi's colleagues lamented the unbecoming decision made by the top executives and the fact that middle management did not object to their superiors. Kiyoshi tried to persuade his colleagues to assemble a group and challenge management to improve its decision-making process. People complained but did not join Kiyoshi in organizing the group to challenge management. Kyoshi's frustration built up so much that he decided to change the course of his own life. He knew that he was limited in challenging management alone. Kiyoshi observed that a few senior managers and executive directors whom he had admired were transferred from Toshiba Headquarters to subsidiaries without their consent. He surmised that they were not in harmony with the decision-making process of the majority of executives.

Upon returning to the Foreign Trade Division, Kiyoshi was assigned as chief of a group in the Third Section. If he challenged his group to work the hardest, the work might not be acknowledged by senior management. How could he take responsibility for his group working the most and not being recognized for their efforts? In the meantime, Kiyoshi could be assigned to another position and leave his group unprotected. He could be transferred anywhere in Toshiba without his consent in the future. Decisions for Kiyoshi's future would be made by someone in the management, and he had no choice but to follow their instruction to accept the next assignment. It was not his intention to work at Toshiba in that way. His initial desire to work at Toshiba was ignored by the management. The only expectation was to take any assignment given to him. These struggles led Kiyoshi to conclude that he should no longer work for Toshiba for the sake of his mental health. He concluded that it was time to leave the company. Kiyoshi was certain that he might face the same problem working at any Japanese company because it was a kind of common culture in the business community in Japan: personal connection in a group, rotational assignment to different divisions, and no professional consideration in management. He decided to continue living in the US after leaving Toshiba. He wanted the value of individualism and self-respect.

Kiyoshi reported to the Foreign Trade Division on December 1, 1965, and told Mr. Yoshihara his decision to leave Toshiba. He was called into the Executive Director's office and commanded to reconsider his decision and come back the next day. Kiyoshi went back to the Executive Director's office the next day and stated that he had not changed his mind. The Executive Director reacted to Kiyoshi's decision personally and dismissed him. Mr. Yoshihara advised Kiyoshi to report his decision to the President of the Toshiba Record Co. (formerly

Executive Vice President in Toshiba Corp., overseeing the Foreign Trade Division) and the manufacturing plant manager in Yamagata Prefecture (formerly Deputy Director of the Foreign Trade Division). Neither was surprised by Kiyoshi's decision and wished him success in the future.

Kiyoshi's decision to leave Toshiba surprised and upset his family, relatives, and friends. They thought Kiyoshi was doing extremely well working at Toshiba. Kiyoshi's brother told him, "Don't give me any problem." One of his uncles said the same. Kiyoshi's friends said he had acted foolishly. Kiyoshi's father told him, "If you are in trouble in the US, just come back to Japan and restart your life."

Soichi and Kiyoshi's mother saw him off at Haneda Airport as he departed for New York via San Francisco on December 27, 1965.

Part IV

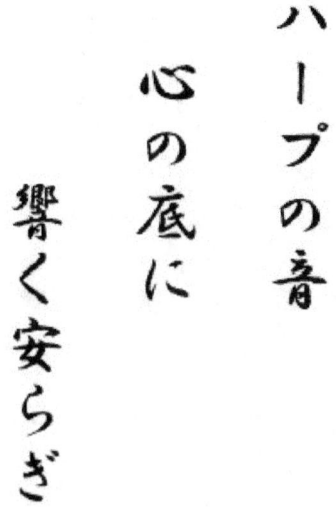

ハープの音
心の底に
響く安らぎ

The tone of the harp

In the bottom of my heart

Humming peace of mind

A gentle quiet

touches softly on my heart—

harp music drifting.

CHAPTER 7
Life with Charlotte Ann (Sheffield) Hamada

The Return to Toshiba America Inc. (TAI)

It took Kiyoshi more than two years to decide to leave Toshiba, and the decision was not an easy one. His future was no longer secure, nor was his promised career for his life. It was a matter of principle for Kiyoshi to make his decision. The meaning of life was still Kiyoshi's main obstacle to clearing his mind. Secular work was a means of economic support for him, but it was never the goal of his life. Challenging himself to complete jobs assigned to him rendered some comfort, but it was not simple for him. The absence of genuine management did not lead the business in a successful direction. The majority of Toshiba executives were just concerned about occupying their positions, not paying attention to improving results. Kiyoshi did not see any future for himself that included a clear conscience when dealing with senior management in Toshiba.

Kiyoshi traveled to Kyoto, advised by his friend, and contracted with the Kyoto Municipal Craft Center as a Trade Advisor. He obtained an E-1 visa sponsored by his acquaintance in New York and secured an apartment at 47 East 83rd Street, New York, NY. He moved to this apartment after his three-year lease ended at the apartment in Riverdale. At this time, he was about six months into his new two-year lease contract. He was ready to live in Manhattan.

Wedding: Charlotte and Kiyoshi, 1967

Kiyoshi had ample time to think about the meaning of life. Zen Buddhism had taught him to cherish life by meditating and awakening his inner nature. Kiyoshi wanted to know more about life and soul relationships. He decided to attend a Christian church, as advised by his friend, and wanted to study the Holy Bible. When he attended a church in uptown East Manhattan, he immediately noticed a young lady attending the same church. She was also part of the same Bible study group. He thought she seemed untouchable, being so popular in the church. He was delighted when she introduced herself to him in a friendly manner. They exchanged names: Charlotte Ann Sheffield and Kiyoshi Hamada. Kiyoshi had more free time, but he was financially very tight. He limited his lunch to a 99-cent sandwich and his supper to a bowl of soup at Soup Burg.

He reported the latest news on the handicraft market in New York to the Kyoto Municipal Craft Center monthly to receive a small trade advisor agent fee. His rent was paid by savings that he brought from Japan. Kiyoshi's friend advised him to apply for a job at the Japan Trade Center, which was a part of JETRO (the overseas agency of MITI of the Japanese government).

Kiyoshi began working at the Japan Trade Center on April 1, 1966. His job in the Business Inquiry Section involved offering Japanese business information to US inquirers. It was not a high-paying job, but it helped Kiyoshi to live a little more decently.

In the meantime, Charlotte and Kiyoshi began getting acquainted with each other and seeing each other more frequently, discussing not only the Bible but also what life is about. Kiyoshi's initial interest in the Holy Bible started from the creation of the universe: the natural environment, the fish in the sea, vegetation, animals on the land, and human life. In Genesis, God (the Creator) intended the perfect creation of human life, then imperfection in life, and finally, restoration to perfection in life. Scientific development has significantly contributed to the high quality of human life, but those were not creations; they were the discovery and use of things on the earth. Charlotte and Kiyoshi talked about these subjects endlessly. They realized that they were developing a mutual interest.

Charlotte was born April 30, 1942, to Mr. and Mrs. Charles W. Sheffield in Fredonia, which was in Chautauqua County in upstate New York. She was an only child and raised in the same town until she graduated from Fredonia High School. She started playing piano at a young age and was a very popular student in her high school. She was interested in writing poems and wanted to be a poet. The Cushing sisters, descendants of Admiral Cushing, were her neighbors and grew fond of Charlotte, accepting her as their child and offering her a lot of advice. It seemed like a very happy life for Charlotte, but she began wondering about living in the small town for her entire life. Most people in town lived their lives like her mother, who was born in Fredonia and remained there for her entire life. Her father came from Florida, settled in Fredonia, and married Charlotte's mother. Charlotte's parents discouraged her from advancing to college. They wanted her to get married to a local boy and settle in the same town, as most people in Fredonia did.

Charlotte wanted to be exposed to more opportunities, experiences, and perhaps higher education. She looked for a sponsor with whom her parents were acquainted in New York City and arranged to get an apartment in Manhattan with some female roommates. Charlotte left for New York City in 1962; coincidentally, the same year Kiyoshi arrived in Manhattan from Japan for the first time. However, they did not meet each other until 1966. Charlotte took a job in an administrative position at a hospital, and her apartment was on Park Avenue, several blocks away from Kiyoshi's apartment on 83rd Street between Madison and Park Avenue. They were living in the same neighborhood. When they began courting, they realized they had so many similarities because Charlotte was an only child, and Kiyoshi was the youngest in the family, often feeling alone. They felt comfort when they were listening to music, walking, talking, and studying the Bible together.

Kiyoshi finally proposed to Charlotte to further their relationship. Charlotte was very talented at dancing of all sorts, but Kiyoshi was not interested in dancing at all. Charlotte was not in favor of Kiyoshi smoking. They made a concession that Kiyoshi would stop smoking (although he was a light smoker), and Charlotte would not ask Kiyoshi to go dancing. This meant that she gave up dancing. They decided to invite Charlotte's parents to a Broadway play and dinner in Manhattan, after a few months of engagement. Kiyoshi approached Charlotte's parents at the dinner table to ask for their consent to marry Charlotte. They were very quiet for a moment, then told Charlotte to go back home with them in upstate NY for further discussion.

Charlotte and Kiyoshi had already decided to get married, no matter what her parents wanted. Charlotte desired to live in a garden apartment to start their married life. They found an apartment in Brooklyn Heights. It was on the first floor with a backyard located on Henry Street, and they signed a one-year lease.

Kiyoshi prepared to leave his apartment to move to Brooklyn Heights before Charlotte came back from upstate New York (possibly with her parents). He placed an ad in the New York Times to sublet his apartment. Several people came to see his apartment immediately because of its highly sought-after location. He selected a person who was working at *The New York Times* and notified the apartment owner's agent.

The day before he was supposed to move out of his apartment, Kiyoshi, coming back from the Japan Trade Center, found that the entrance door to his apartment was broken, and the inside had been ransacked. The apartment was on the fourth floor of a brownstone building with steel doors at both the main entrance and each apartment. Both steel doors (the entrance and Kiyoshi's) were broken, possibly by a crowbar. He and the police surmised that someone who came to see his apartment through the ad in *The New York Times* might have been the culprit. He lost most of his electronics and his buckskin jacket. The police asked Kiyoshi the total value in dollars of his stolen items.

Charlotte somehow persuaded her parents to let her marry Kiyoshi. Friends in her hometown threw her a bridal party. Charlotte and Kiyoshi set a wedding date and decided to have the ceremony at their apartment. Charlotte and her parents came to their new apartment the day before the wedding. The apartment was almost empty except for the bed. The pre-ordered furniture has not been delivered yet. Kiyoshi had to stay overnight at his friend's place in Manhattan before the wedding day. Many of Charlotte's friends from her hometown and some of Kiyoshi's friends from New York City came to celebrate the wedding. A reverend performed the wedding ceremony in the backyard of the apartment on May 27, 1967. All visitors left the apartment after the wedding party, leaving Charlotte and Kiyoshi alone.

The newly married couple did not plan to go on a honeymoon immediately after the wedding. A lack of funds made them stay home, and instead, they looked forward to having their honeymoon in the near future. A year later, they went to the Cayman Islands for their honeymoon, but they were accompanied by Charlotte's parents.

Fishing in Cayman Islands, 1968

Kiyoshi went back to work the next day, while Charlotte sent cards of gratitude to all visitors to the wedding. Most of the items for the new apartment were purchased on credit. Charlotte said," We are starting zero minus." Charlotte had the option of marrying a more financially secure person than Kiyoshi. There was no doubt that Charlotte struggled with her decision to choose her husband among her boyfriends. As a matter of fact, she was engaged to a high school classmate who was from the wealthiest family in her hometown. She broke off their engagement and returned the engagement ring to him after she decided to choose Kiyoshi. Charlotte wanted Kiyoshi to meet her boyfriends one by one before her decision, without telling them why.

Charlotte began taking temporary jobs to help their financial situation. They were in high spirits, regardless of being broke. They talked and walked around Hudson Bay whenever they had time together. Kiyoshi gave up his car when he moved to Manhattan, so the couple took an overnight bus to visit Charlotte's parents, leaving on Friday night and returning early Monday morning to their apartment. Kiyoshi became acquainted not only with Charlotte's parents but also their family friends.

Charlotte was concerned about Kiyoshi's physical condition because he was so skinny (less than one hundred pounds). She visited Kiyoshi's doctor in Manhattan and consulted with him on how Kiyoshi could improve his physical condition (dropped stomach). The doctor told Charlotte, "Do not worry about him, but nourish him, providing every meal by yourself. He will be fine after he gains weight." She began cooking at home and obtained a variety of cookbooks. The doctor's suggestion worked. Kiyoshi gradually gained weight, and his stomach problem was solved.

Great Swamp National Wildlife Refuge in Morristown, NJ

When Charlotte and Kiyoshi were talking on the porch, facing the backyard, after they got back home from work in late March 1968, Kiyoshi received a phone call from TAI asking him to meet them. Kiyoshi was surprised that

TAI had his phone number because he had never contacted anyone there since leaving Toshiba. He was not interested in contacting them, although he did not have any hard feelings. Charlotte suggested that Kiyoshi meet them. He reluctantly agreed to meet them in their office. Kiyoshi paid a visit to the TAI office on Madison Avenue in Manhattan the next day. Mr. Takamiya, now President of TAI, who had shown care for Kiyoshi as the head of Human Resources at Toshiba Headquarters when Kiyoshi left the company, offered him a job at TAI. He even said that he wanted Kiyoshi to take care of TAI for a lengthy period and become the Vice President one day. Kiyoshi was still reluctant to accept his offer , but finally accepted on the condition that he would not be assigned to work in sales and marketing, nor work in a different location without his consent. Mr. Takamiya accepted Kiyoshi's request and told him to start working at TAI on April 1, 1968. Charlotte was delighted at Kiyoshi's acceptance of this job offer. Kiyoshi knew that his job at the Japan Trade Center was not a career, though he had been promoted to head of the Business Inquiry Section, because he was not a Japanese government employee.

Brooklyn Heights: In front of the apartment where Charlotte and Kiyoshi lived for 6 years

Charlotte and Kiyoshi started to look for another apartment before their lease term was over and found an ideal apartment on Willow Street, a quieter and strictly residential area in *where Charlotte and Kiyoshi lived for 6 years* Brooklyn Heights. They contracted a three-year lease for a garden apartment, sharing a backyard with the building owner, Mr. and Mrs. Tom

111

Gallagher. Charlotte and Kiyoshi began to feel settled in their lives. They started renting a car to go around Long Island on weekends, which eventually stretched to include traveling to the Shenandoah Mountains in Virginia and to Portland, Maine. They had to watch their spending, but they enjoyed each other's adventurous spirit. The "zero-minus" situation did not stop them from taking venturesome action. They also encouraged each other in studying the Bible and put their minds together. Charlotte had to limit working for a long time because her stamina did not allow her to continue working. She needed to take a break to restore her energy.

Some of the jobs Charlotte took included an administrator role in hospitals, the New Product Development Division of Clinique in Estee Lauder, the Council on Foreign Relations (publisher of Foreign Affairs), and an administrative position at a private medical doctor's office in uptown East Manhattan.

In the meantime, Charlotte and Kiyoshi decided to look for an apartment in Manhattan to cut down their commute time after living in Brooklyn Heights for seven years. They found an apartment on the seventh floor at 12 East 97th Street, around the corner from Fifth Avenue. They started to be exposed to a different life, becoming members of the New York Metropolitan Museum of Art, the National Historic Museum, the Japan Society, and more. They walked around the water reservoir in Central Park during the daytime and along Fifth Avenue at midnight. Kiyoshi tried encouraging Charlotte to extend her education. She began attending New York University, the New School to study business administration, and Columbia University to study Japanese and Old English. She fulfilled her interests by attending classes and receiving the Paralegal Certificate from New York University in June 1978.

Kiyoshi had plenty of time, commuting by subway from Brooklyn Heights to Manhattan and then Manhattan to Flushing, Queens, and decided to read the Holy Bible on the subway. He wanted to know the whole concept of the Bible, so he started to read from Genesis to Revelation, page by page. He completed reading the Bible twice by the time he started driving his own car instead of commuting by subway.

Charlotte walked in to apply for an audition at Juilliard School of Music without any preparation. She passed the audition unexpectedly but declined the offer to be a student. She was not interested in getting into Juilliard School of Music, but she wanted to know how her piano playing would be evaluated by the school since she had had private tutors throughout her childhood who taught her how to play piano.

Uptown East Manhattan

When TAI Headquarters moved from Manhattan to Wayne, New Jersey, Kiyoshi had to buy an automobile to commute to the TAI office. Getting a car made it easier to visit Charlotte's parents, leaving the apartment at midnight on Friday, arriving at Charlotte's parents' house early Saturday morning, and getting back to their apartment by midnight on Sunday. It took them six to seven hours of driving in each direction.

Heavy snow in uptown Manhattan

Charlotte's health condition began worsening. She developed low blood sugar. One night, Kiyoshi took Charlotte to the emergency room at nearby Mt. Sinai Hospital for treatment when she felt like her heart was failing. A doctor advised Charlotte to drink a glass of Coca-Cola. Living in a big city like Manhattan had finally caught up with her, as she had been raised in a rather quiet, small suburban town in upstate New York.

They realized it was time to move out of Manhattan to a place where they could live in a quiet, natural environment for two reasons. One was for Charlotte's health, and the other was to reduce Kiyoshi's commute from Manhattan to Wayne, NJ. They decided to look for a house at this time in northern New Jersey. A real estate agent went out on a limb after introducing them to many houses in northern New Jersey and showed them one last choice. Charlotte and Kiyoshi were attracted to the secluded five-acre property, with easy access to a grocery shopping area and a reasonable distance for Kiyoshi to commute to TAI. They liked the idea of working on an unfinished house and its surrounding property. The real estate agent could not believe they decided to take that kind of property, having labeled them as city people.

Charlotte's dog

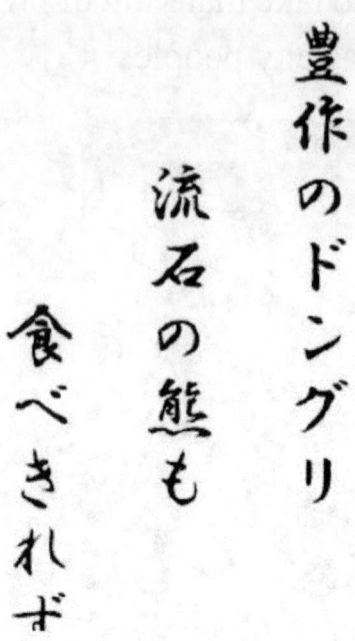

Acorns of a good harvest

even bear

could not eat them all

Even the bear

cannot finish all the acorns in this rich harvest.

Charlotte and Kiyoshi began their new life, moving into a house in Sussex County, NJ, on April 1, 1985. Charlotte's health was still not good enough to get around the new property easily. The driveway to the house from the street was one-tenth of a mile uphill. She could not walk forward up the hill, but had to go backward. She decided not to obtain a New Jersey driver's license after driving her car for a while with her New York driver's license. She said that she did not like people's driving behavior.

Reconfirmation by Episcopal Dioceses and local Reverend

The natural environment began to help Charlotte recover her health gradually. She started working outdoors—clearing leaves, picking up broken branches, weeding, and shoveling snow from the driveway in the winter— in addition to cooking at home. She stayed home most of the time and fulfilled her interests by reading page by page from A to Z in the encyclopedia. Kiyoshi not only worked long days, but he also took business trips very often, so Charlotte had plenty of time alone at home. Whenever they had time together, they worked on fixing the house and went out for dinner. When Kiyoshi took vacation days, they traveled not only to Charlotte's parents' area but also to the southern states. They visited historical sites via an inland route to Florida, visiting interesting places and towns. Charlotte initiated the idea of traveling to these places, and Kiyoshi made concrete plans for hotel reservations and the entire travel itinerary.

Cumberland, MD, with Charlotte's parents

Charlotte and Kiyoshi

Sometimes Kiyoshi was accompanied by Charlotte on his business trips to Japan, paying for her airfare out of their pocket money and asking his family to take diligent care of her. Kiyoshi's eldest sister, Masako, took Charlotte to the Izu Peninsula. They got along without speaking English, relying on body language and a Japanese/English dictionary. After completing his business assignment with Toshiba, Kiyoshi took extra days off and traveled with Charlotte to Kyoto and Nara. They were relaxed, just two of them, in the atmosphere of a peaceful and cultural environment. They stretched their adventurous travel to Ueno, Shiga Prefecture, where the birthplace of poet Matsuo Basho was located, and the Ninja citadel had stood in the old days. Charlotte had regained her health enough to go on these trips in addition to doing domestic work.

Kiyoshi's mother, brother's family, and Charlotte in brother's house

Charlotte and Kiyoshi commemorated their 25th wedding anniversary in August 1992 with a ceremony of thanksgiving and blessing for their marriage at the Church of the Heavenly Rest on Fifth Avenue in New York City. The service included communion and a reaffirmation of their wedding vows. The officiant was the Rev. C. Hugh Hildesley, accompanied by the Rev. John J. Lloyd, an Episcopal missionary for the Metropolitan Japanese Missionary, sponsored by the Diocese of New Jersey, New York City, and Long Island.

A reception following the ceremony was held in the library of Heavenly Church. A Shakuhachi flutist and a koto vocalist performed music. Friends of Charlotte and Kiyoshi participated in this memorial occasion.

25th wedding anniversary party after official ceremony performed by Rev. Hugh Hildesley and Rev. John Lloyd

Their happy marriage continued when Kiyoshi retired from Toshiba America Consumer Products Inc. on May 1, 1998. They were relieved from external pressures and felt liberated, able to plan their own activities at any time. They planned to take a trip to Europe to visit Charlotte's friend in Vienna, Austria, and then take a train to Budapest, Hungary, Switzerland, and Italy.

Another trip was to take Amtrak from coast to coast on the northern corridor to San Francisco via Chicago for sightseeing, with a one-day stopover at Portland, Oregon. They would then fly to Tokyo via Honolulu, Hawaii, staying for a few days. They attended the wedding ceremony and reception of Kiyoshi's niece at the International House of Japan and traveled to Kyoto for some relaxation. They took a flight to visit Hawaii again for a few days, then flew to Los Angeles to meet Charlotte's cousin, and finally took the central corridor of Amtrak to get back home.

They were together almost all the time. Charlotte buried her father in 1998. She and Kiyoshi tried to comfort Charlotte's mother as a widow by visiting almost monthly, driving four hundred miles one-way to Charlotte's mother's house and later to her assisted living facility. Charlotte began to lose her physical strength but refused to be examined by any doctor, no matter how many times Kiyoshi's doctors offered.

Charlotte wanted to go to a classical music concert at the Wilmington Hotel in Wilmington, Delaware, regardless of having difficulty moving around. Kiyoshi had to use the hotel's wheelchair. That was the last time she was able to be out of the house.

Charlotte could not leave her bed for two weeks and still refused to submit herself to any doctor. She finally told Kiyoshi she needed emergency admission to a hospital. Kiyoshi arranged a private ambulance to take her to Morristown Memorial Hospital, where his doctors were affiliated. She was taken to the emergency room immediately and examined thoroughly. Doctors in the emergency department decided to transfer Charlotte to the Simon Building for cancer treatment. Her physical status was so weak that the hospital hesitated to conduct a surgical procedure. Kiyoshi insisted on attending the doctor's meeting to discuss how to treat Charlotte. A chief doctor explained that it was impossible because doctors corresponded mostly by phone conversation or exchanged emails. Kiyoshi stayed in Charlotte's room overnight for a month and a half until she passed away on January 28, 2018. It had been over fifty years of married life together, and Charlotte had been preparing for their golden anniversary event. But she lost her life before the celebration could take place.

Charlotte and Kiyoshi had secured a gravesite at Somerset Memorial Park in Morris County as soon as they settled in Sussex County, NJ, in 1985. But Charlotte had also wanted to be buried beside her parents in her hometown. Kiyoshi decided her body would be cremated and received two urns to bury in two grave sites. The memorial service at Charlotte's gravesite in her hometown was eulogized by the local judge, who had been Charlotte's classmate at Fredonia High School. Charlotte's many friends and acquaintances came to pay their respects. Cars driven by attendees of the memorial service were lined up all the way to the entrance of the cemetery. Kiyoshi invited all attendees to a catered memorial dinner at Chautauqua Country Golf Club following the service. Many people talked about Charlotte at the gravesite and dinner table—sharing how she had been a kind and thoughtful person.

A little over fifty years of married life was gone. Numerous memories came back one after another, but the reality of being together was gone. The twenty-some years after Kiyoshi had retired were the most fruitful time in his relationship with Charlotte. They did have some disagreements and arguments, but they took time to cool off and look for solutions to compromise with each other. They did everything together and accommodated many visitors; Charlotte's parents, her friends from her hometown, Kiyoshi's family and his friends from Japan, and their mutual friends, with whom they had barbecues in the backyard and stayed overnight. Most of those people were aged by the time Charlotte had health issues.

When Kiyoshi began pursuing his retirement, he realized a few critical issues needed to be solved. Charlotte was seven years younger than Kiyoshi, so it was natural to expect that Kiyoshi may pass away before her.

Reasonably comfortable financial readiness to support Charlotte for the rest of her life without Kiyoshi must be established. A continuation of Kiyoshi's Japanese citizenship may have caused complications in settling legal procedures between the Japanese Inheritance Law and US law, regardless of a written will. Kiyoshi had already declared his intention to prepare a retirement fund when he reached fifty years old. As to the citizenship issue, Kiyoshi decided to become a US citizen to simplify the legality.

Kiyoshi became a US citizen in 1997, one year before his retirement. Business associates, an attorney at law, and investment advisors grew worried about Charlotte's physical and mental status. Charlotte began talking incoherently to them at the meeting after her health problems became noticeable. They were concerned about how to work with her if Kiyoshi passed away. Charlotte may have had a difficult situation managing her daily life without her driver's license and communication issues with her business associates. It may have been difficult for her to survive. But in reality, it was Kiyoshi who was left alone!

Kiyoshi was having difficulty living in the same house where he and Charlotte had lived together for so long, but he had no intention of giving up their house. He decided to deviate from his living circumstances for a while. Kiyoshi, assisted by his nephew Naoki, rented an apartment in Tokyo for three months. Kiyoshi had a flourishing time meeting his family and friends, strolling the streets in Tokyo alone, and taking a trip with his friends to visit Kiyosato in Yamanashi Prefecture. His mind was reset by the time he returned home, and he was ready to live as a widower in the same house.

Part V

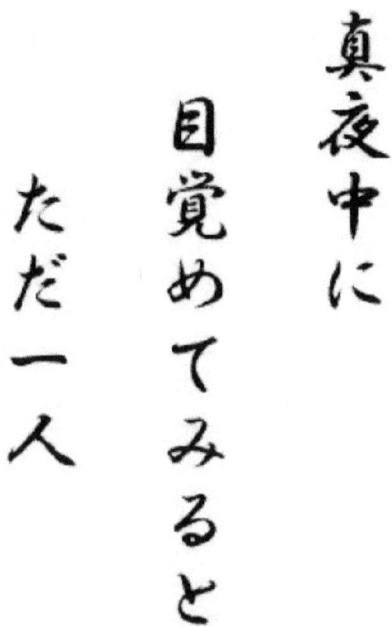

真夜中に
目覚めてみると
ただ一人

In the middle of night

When I wake up

I am only one

I realized I am the only person when I woke up
in the middle of the night.

CHAPTER 8
Introducing Computer Systems to Toshiba America Inc.

The Return to TAI

Kiyoshi reported to TAI on Madison Avenue on April 1, 1968. He was now a local employee. It was a different status of employment, a different payroll, and second-class treatment.

He determined to concentrate on his work to be done. His first assignment was to work with Underwriters Laboratories (UL Solutions) for TAI to obtain safety certification on Toshiba products. Bulky products were sent to UL directly from Toshiba in Japan. Kyoshi contacted UL to follow up and supplied extra engineering information upon request from UL. He traveled by car to the UL office in Connecticut for personal contact and carried additional small-sized products for their tests. It was not the kind of job Kiyoshi had expected to do at TAI as part of his career, but he knew a better assignment would come to him soon, which was anticipated with the introduction of computer systems to TAI. There was no curriculum on computer science at Keio University when he was there, but he had already been involved in the preparation of introducing computer systems at Toshiba, as stated before. Everybody at Toshiba—not just those in the accounting departments—used an abacus to handle figures. A skill-based aptitude contest for using an abacus was one of the company-wide events. TAI had a hand-driven calculator for local accounting personnel. Typists typed letters and documents, including invoices. The formal communication to Tokyo was through handwritten documents sent by US mail. Carbon copies were kept in files. Daily communication with Tokyo was conducted via a telex machine, alphabetically typed for Japanese expression. The copy machine used a photosensitive paper, which was phased out shortly.

Introduction of Computer Systems to TAI

TAI began increasing its sales volume of consumer electronics in the US market. The administration started struggling with processing paperwork manually and obtaining the results of daily sales activities. It was then that TAI management asked Kiyoshi to prepare for the introduction of a computer system for TAI operations. Kiyoshi began setting up a coding structure for products, product categories, customer numbers, customer categories, sales representatives, states, branches, and so on.

He began taking an IBM programming class on how to wire on boards and became ready to introduce the first IBM machine to TAI in December 1968. Kiyoshi hired two keypunchers, who keyed from typewritten invoices to produce punched cards. Kiyoshi then processed punched cards on an IBM 403 to generate daily and monthly sales reports for management. This accounting machine was equipped with electron tubes and type sets for printing, along with a wiring board to manipulate data from punched cards. The life of electron tubes was very short, and the type sets tended to get jammed. The IBM service person carried a hammer, soldering tools, electron tubes, and type sets. One technician was assigned to work in a commercial building in Manhattan. Kiyoshi kept some electron tubes and type sets in his desk drawer. The sorter and collator were to organize punched cards, but those machines had a tendency to jam during the process.

The IBM 403 with a cam was capable of adding, subtracting, multiplying, and dividing with no memory capacity. Kiyoshi wired a board to handle electrical pulses by processing punched cards from shipment documents as the data source for printing invoices and credit memos, while simultaneously generating punch cards for sales and accounts receivable. The wired board that performed all these processes got so heavy that it weighed over thirty pounds.

The IBM 360/20, the first computer with 32 kilobytes of memory based on a punch card system, was installed in April 1970. Kiyoshi began preparing a new operating system by learning RPG language in an IBM class, enabling him to generate invoices and credit memos through punched cards from shipment/return documents. As a byproduct, the system generated punched cards of sales and accounts receivable records. He had to replace all the processes, from wiring on a board to software programming. The main challenge of this programming was how to compact the RPG source program to generate punched cards for an object program within its limited memory capacity (32k). Repeatedly processing the reprogrammed source deck (punched cards) over and over to be able to generate object program cards within the 32k memory capacity was quite time-consuming. It turned out that punch card table applications and the proper use of indicators compensated for the lack of memory capacity.

TAI had sales branches in Los Angeles and Chicago. Consolidated sales reports, including branch operations, were basic tools for sales management at TAI. Kiyoshi introduced billing machines at branches in Los Angeles and later in Chicago to produce invoices and credit memos while simultaneously generating punched cards of sales/accounts receivable records. Each branch sent its punched cards at the end of the day to the Data Processing Department in New York by overnight US mail. The Data Processing Department processed all punched cards, including those generated by the New York Branch, to produce TAI's daily sales reports in the morning and sent them to management by noon every day. Various monthly sales reports and accounts receivable reports were produced at the end of each month.

The profit/loss situation of TAI's operations became a serious issue. Management decided to restructure every area of the company. TAI Headquarters was relocated from

Manhattan to Flushing, Queens. The Data Processing Department (already operating in Flushing) was no exception to this restructuring. Kiyoshi had to respond to this request by changing the computer system. There was no excuse to reduce the productivity of data processing because of restructuring.

Kiyoshi decided to introduce a computer system with higher productivity and reduced manpower requirements. He selected IBM System 3 Model 6, equipped with disk drives that had telecommunication capability and one-person operation. Ten keypunchers and computer operators lost their jobs. Kiyoshi had to prepare new programs to operate the IBM S/3/6 in 1973 and trained his secretary to be a data entry operator. Kiyoshi also programmed new billing machines capable of remote operation with a teleprocessing function. He visited branch offices to install the new billing machines, negotiating with local telephone companies for near noise-free lines capable of sending batch data to the IBM S/3/6 in Flushing. No more overnight US mail of punched cards!

One day, the Senior Vice President of Toshiba Corp. visited TAI's operations, when Kiyoshi was working in Flushing. He happened to be the Executive Director of the Foreign Trade Division when Kiyoshi left Toshiba, and now he oversaw the sales administration of Toshiba Corp. He started to talk to Kiyoshi alone, asking him to return to Toshiba Corp. and help improve sales and marketing at Headquarters. He knew why Kiyoshi had left Toshiba, and he got upset at Kiyoshi's departure at that time. Now, he was asking Kiyoshi to rejoin Toshiba. Kiyoshi smiled and did not respond to his request.

As TAI resumed increasing its sales activity, the number of sales branches grew. TAI Headquarters was relocated back to Manhattan. Telecommunication had become a very important means of data processing for computer operations. The upgrading of computer systems to meet expanded TAI's sales operations was unavoidable. The Data Processing Department changed the computer system practically every two years to respond to

TAI's growing business operations. The introduction of the IBM S/3/15B-D in 1977–1982 was still a batch processing operation, but it increased data communication capability. Kiyoshi alone prepared modified software programs to operate the IBM S/15B-D. The IBM Series 1, which operated with the ASCI language, was added to S/3/15D, helped by an IBM special systems engineer in 1979. The IBM Series 1 had seven communication ports to handle receiving batch data from seven different locations at once. All seven sales branches did not need to wait for the other branches to complete batch data transactions to the IBM S/3/15D.

When TAI decided to set up an assembly line to produce phonographs in New York, Kiyoshi set up a Bill of Materials system, which included purchase orders for components and inventory management of components from production plans. Three levels of the manufacturing process worked well.

The phonograph engineer helped Kiyoshi modify the S/3/15D to shut down the system by using a set timer. The modification made it possible for a timer to shut down the circuits sequentially, closing all files in the system. It worked well so that the computer operator did not need to stay with the computer until Los Angeles finished its data transactions for the night. IBM did not recommend the S/3/15D be kept on all night without supervision. It was a crazy time for Kiyoshi, working with only one computer operator and one secretary. As soon as he finished the new programming, punched on mylar tape for the billing machines, in addition to programming for the computer systems, he visited all branches to introduce the operation of the new billing machine to designated operators in the sales branch office. People from the IBM New York office and AT&T were eminently supportive of Kiyoshi's efforts.

TAI Headquarters moved its office from Manhattan to Wayne, New Jersey, in 1982, to be reasonably functional for the growth of the business. The brand-new building with a warehouse was well-suited for its sales activities. The Data Processing Department was expanding its programming staff, not only to support distribution systems, but also to develop accounting systems, credit systems, and services for parts and repairs.

When IBM announced the System 38 in 1982, TAI was fully liberated from batch teleprocessing and introduced online operations. IBM underwent an internal restructuring that affected TAI. IBM's New York branch office announced that it was no longer able to support TAI because it would be limited to servicing only customers in New York City. This was during the transition from the S/3/15D to the System 38. The System 38 was an innovative computer, unlike the System 3 series. Its database provision unlocked easy access to computer data for its users without programming, and enabled PC users to download computer data for their spreadsheets. IBM system engineers were willing to continue working with TAI. They were quite familiar with TAI's computer application system, having worked with the company for more than ten years.

Kiyoshi consulted with the Legal Department and decided to write a letter to the President of IBM stating the crucial situation of the system conversion in TAI. He emphasized that losing a productive relationship with IBM's system engineers from the New York branch was unacceptable, because IBM is under restructuring. A Branch Manager of IBM's New York office visited Kiyoshi a week later, promising him that the office would continue supporting TAI, regardless of the restructuring or territorial issues.

Sears Roebuck & Co. developed its own privately standardized data format to exchange computer data with its business associates by eliminating printed documents, like purchase orders and other related documents, that needed to be mail to them. The SENDEN system was introduced, and Sears requested TAI to join in this computer data transaction, receiving purchase orders from Sears. Sears had long been a retailer of Toshiba color televisions in its stores. Kiyoshi met with Sears' computer systems people who visited TAI in Wayne and the Sears Tower in Chicago to further discuss computer data formats and procedures for batch data teleprocessing. This relationship continued until the US business industry introduced Electronic Data Interchange (EDI), which was the standardized computer data transaction format between business entities.

Sales and marketing management emphasized increasing sales volume by offering customers all sorts of incentives. It became complicated because salespeople could offer all sorts of incentives to customers, but could not show the net price because of the many discounts. They were only interested in getting purchase orders from their customers. Salespeople were awarded an annual bonus based on the sales amount, so they, working with their customers, often held off returning merchandise until the beginning of the next fiscal year to inflate sales records. Top executives inflated their sales achievements to the Headquarters in Tokyo. They then blamed Toshiba Headquarters for their negative profit/loss results due to a lack of cost-cutting efforts in manufacturing. The Data Processing Department was responsible for supporting all these complicated sales practices by implementing capable computer systems.

The lineup of Toshiba products started to increase. Multiple divisions in Toshiba began marketing their products through TAI. These included personal computers, copy machines, medical equipment, industrial motors, electrical power generators for power plants, semiconductors, electron tubes, microwave ovens, dry-cell batteries, and so on, in addition to the main consumer products. The variety of marketing processes according to the product line required different computer processes and application programs.

CHAPTER 9
Toshiba America
Consumer Products Inc.

Expansion of business practices of various divisional products in the US market by TAI led Toshiba Headquarters to reorganize, setting up five subsidiary companies that represented each manufacturing division in Toshiba. TAI became the shareholding company of these five subsidiary companies. Four of five subsidiaries, except Toshiba America Consumer Products Inc. (TACP), established corporate locations on the West Coast. Kiyoshi preferred to stay with TACP in Wayne, New Jersey.

TACP appointed Kiyoshi Vice President in charge of Information Systems on April 1, 1985. Kiyoshi prepared to transfer all related coding and data to these subsidiaries. Since TACP had a core computer system, he coordinated the computer installations in all TAI subsidiaries. Some subsidiaries planned to install mainframe computers, and others planned to install UNISYS. Kiyoshi visited all subsidiaries and persuaded them to install IBM midrange computers so they could interface with each other smoothly. He also arranged for IBM and AT&T to serve all TAI subsidiaries without local differences.

TACP Executive Party: Kiyoshi was promoted to Vice President

Executive IOS Class by IBM 1987

TACP had manufacturing plants in Tennessee and Mexico, a Toshiba Hawaii sales office, and TACP sales branches. The chassis of color televisions were assembled in Mexico and sent to the Tennessee plant for the final assembly. The Central Service and Distribution Centers were located within a part of the Tennessee manufacturing plant facility. The lineup of merchandise offered by TACP included color televisions, VCRs, cordless telephone sets, audio products, cell phones, microwave ovens, and dry-cell batteries. The foremost items were color televisions, followed by VCRs. There were twenty competing color television providers in the US market at that time.

A telephone call to Kiyoshi, who was representing the Society for Information Management (SIM), invited him to be one of the speakers at SIM's 1988 Annual National Conference in Minneapolis, Minnesota. SIM was the most prestigious information management organization in the United States. The organization sent Kiyoshi a preliminary program for the conference, listing him as a speaker, along with the President of Apple, the CEO of MCI, the CEO of Gray, and others. SIM expected attendants at the conference to be in the range of 400 to 500 people, including various company information system executives, academics from major universities, and business executives. Kiyoshi realized that SIM was expecting him to represent Toshiba Corp., so he decided to get approval from Toshiba Headquarters through the Chairman of TAI. Toshiba executives concluded that Kiyoshi should not be a speaker at the SIM conference. Their concern was that Toshiba was in the midst of a case involving a violation of COCOM by its subsidiary, Toshiba Machine Co., in the United States. The attitude of Toshiba executives was very negative. Kiyoshi, to the contrary, believed that it was an opportunity to state Toshiba's firm policies and fair business practices in the United States. That was, however, Toshiba Headquarters' final decision, and he had to comply. Kiyoshi regretfully declined the invitation from SIM but accepted an offer to join as a member.

Sales meetings and executive meetings at TACP focused on increasing revenue by lowering prices to remain competitive in the US market. Sales management often compared pricing to that of lesser competitors and insisted on giving more discounts to dealers and distributors. Kiyoshi questioned at the meeting why TACP did not initiate its own advertisement to consumers through media, highlighting Toshiba's quality products, instead of giving discounts to dealers and distributors. Toshiba, as a manufacturer, was in an advantageous position to produce higher-quality, better-engineered products. Toshiba had already established that reputation among consumers. Sales/marketing and top management were mostly interested in increasing revenue rather than profit/loss figures. They preferred to demonstrate to Toshiba Headquarters that they could expand to a larger scale of business.

Toshiba decided to outsource consumer products to manufacturers in foreign countries and closed its own manufacturing plants in Japan, the United States, Mexico, and elsewhere after pressure came from sales/marketing over pricing issues. This was a serious decision for the manufacturer. Since Toshiba had an advantageous position in engineering and product development, the company should have continued striving to produce superior merchandise instead of placing Toshiba in a pricing competition with other competitors. This was a failure of an executive decision-making. Toshiba ultimately lost its position in the market and, furthermore, lost its manufacturing operations. A long history of pioneering Toshiba consumer products was abolished by a handful of executives who emphasized short-term business expansion without a long-term plan.

The Information Systems Department was a supporting department for TACP's sales activity. It was responsible for providing services for TCAP operations. Once a decision was made, the Information Systems Department had to make every effort to function in support of TCAP's operations, as long as it was ethical and productive.

I/S hardware configuration

AS/400 Model F60 1

AS/400 Model F45 2

AS/400 Model F10 2

ECS Modem 5853/001 4

ECS Modem 7855/V.35 1

System Printer 6262/014 1

Rack Enclosure 9309/002 2

Disk Unit 9337/010 2

Disk Unit 9337/020 3

Magnetic Tape Subsystem 9348/001 1

Magnetic Tape Subsystem 9394/L10 1

Remote Communication Control Unit

5394/01C 2

Remote Communication Control Unit

5494/002 1

The above configuration includes the main computer system, data communication network, client-server, and LAN. The manufacturing sites in Tennessee and Mexico were not included.

The coordination between TACP I/S and I/S of manufacturing sites is stated on the following page.

	P R O G R E S S		
	TRP-IS	TRP-IS	TAKF-IS
I. Issues for Coordination			
Budget			
Expense	preliminary proposal	preliminary proposal	final proposal
Headcount	preliminary proposal	preliminary proposal	final proposal
Legal Contract	proposal	proposal	finalization
IS Status Survey (plan/status)	preparation	preparation	finalization
Hardware/Software Aquisition and/or Cancellation	proposal	proposal	issue orders to vendor
Telecommunication	proposal	proposal	finalization
Short/Long-term Project Plan	preliminary plan	preliminary plan	final proposal
Activity Status Report (monthly)	issue	issue	review
Support on IS Activities (include technical consultation)	exchange	exchange	exchange
II. Issues for Individual IS Responsibility			
Systems Development and Maintenance	expedite	expedite	expedite
Systems Operations	expedite	expedite	expedite
Documentation	expedite	expedite	expedite
Day to day Personnel Management	expedite	expedite	expedite
User Training and Education	expedite	expedite	expedite

Professional Development

The installation of the AS/400 in January 1989 provided a full scope of computer capabilities to TACP: productivity of system development, data security, data communication network, network security, client-server, and so on. New policies and procedures were provided for members of the Information Systems Department.

Project Management oversaw the project and its procedures: organizing project teams, establishing system design, estimating system delivery, checking the progress of system development, finalizing system delivery to users, preparing system documentation and user manuals, and providing follow-up care to system users. Most computer systems were developed in-house, except for accounting and payroll.

Policies and Procedures

Computer systems became an essential supporting function for practically every department in TACP. Computer users and the Information Systems Department worked together to develop computer systems, which were essential for completing projects effectively. Policies and procedures issued by the Information Systems Department were essential to work with both parties on a common ground. The client-server model expanded to all PC users, who were required to understand the scope of responsibilities the Information Systems Department was involved in. People who worked in TACP had a variety of backgrounds and ideas. Providing Policies and Procedures placed everyone on common ground to work together.

The Information Systems Department remained open and neutral, working with all kinds of system users. The professionalism of the Information Systems Department required ethical conduct.

On one occasion, a request came from the Treasurer asking the Information System Department to modify data in the database before the IRS audit team examined the business practices of TACP. The company had obviously double-booked financial reports for the US and Toshiba Corp. in Japan. Kiyoshi refused his request, saying that the Information Systems Department had to maintain accurate records of TACP's activity. No one could modify any records in the database. The Treasurer became so mad that he told everyone that Kiyoshi was uncooperative and gave him a terrible evaluation.

Kiyoshi was open with all the audit teams from the IRS and the state taxation office, responding to any requests for records from the Information Systems database. He believed that TACP should pay any penalties if they had committed a wrongdoing instead of covering it up. The head of Human Resources came to Kiyoshi, asking what was going on between him and the Treasurer. Kiyoshi smiled and did not say anything.

When a new President was assigned to TACP from Toshiba Corp., Kiyoshi requested that the Information Systems Department report to the President instead of to the Treasurer. After explaining the above incident to a newly assigned Treasurer from Toshiba Corp., the President changed the organization chart so that the Information Systems Department reported to him.

Access to the physical files of the database was limited to the management of the Information Systems Department. Programmers and other staff were limited to working with a virtual file separated by a partition.

Information Systems Policy

1. Clarify full business vision and strategy.

2. Develop a conceptual system design to achieve its vision.

3. Promote Computer Integrated Sales/Manufacturing System (CISM)

4. Minimize investment, deliver timely, and achieve better performance on system development and maintenance.

5. Define roles and responsibilities as an Information Systems charter.

Standard Procedure

- System development and programming

- Project management

- Naming convention

- Programming standard

- Documentation

- Client-based coordination

- PC management

- Help desk

- User manual

- General announcement

- Data communication and network

- Online (T1, Frame Relay, X.25, Switched)

- File transfer (EDI)

- LAN

- Database management

- Production system (transaction data)

- Information database (end-user computing)

- EIS

- Security and control

- Office automation

- Auditing

- Accounting audit

- Tax audit (IRS and state government)

- Third-party audit

- Toshiba audit

- Quality control

- Productivity

System Concepts

The core system development at TACP was a distribution system, which was designed for highly complex sales practices. These include price discounts from the list price, different pricing for different categorized customers, seasonal promotional pricing, volume discounts, Co-Ad, and over 120 different payment terms. It was impossible to show net prices when sales/marketing offered a variety of discounts to customers. Only the invoice generated the net prices according to predetermined discount programs. The Accounting and Credit Departments could not figure out cash flow because of these complex payment terms. The Information Systems Department was in the position of developing whatever system requirements were set by the top management, as long as it was technically possible. System planning, system design, and all application software, except the accounting system and payroll, were developed by the Information Systems Department without external consultants' fees or commercial software packages. Arthur Andersen Consulting tried to sell its software package to replace TACP's in-house developed distribution systems. A partner from Arthur Andersen System Consulting concluded that TACP's in-house systems were the most suitable systems for the company's operations, after analyzing all aspects of it. The Accounting Department requested JD Edwards's accounting package to replace the in-house developed accounting system and contracted Arthur Andersen Consulting to train them in how to use it. The Information Systems Department worked on interfacing this package with the TACP database.

Data communication, client service, and office automation were essential for TACP's operations. TACP sometimes exported its products to various countries, so export control systems became an additional important process.

The number of customers with EDI transactions increased to thirty-three accounts. Transaction types included purchase orders, purchase order changes, order status inquiries, invoices, credit memos, credit approvals, remittance advice, shipment notices, inventory availability inquiries, purchase forecasts, product activities, text messages, planning schedules, payment transfers, and miscellaneous correspondence.

TACP INFORMATION SYSTEM CONCEPT

```
PURCHASE              DISTRIBUTION        CREDIT             SERVICE        WARRANTY
ORDER                 SYSTEM              CONTROL            PARTS          CLAIM
                                          SYSTEM                            PROCESS
(PRODUCT)             ------------                           ----------
                      ORDER PROCESS       ------------       P/O
SHIPPING              RETURN              ACCOUNTS           ORDER
ADVICE                MS/MC               RECEIVABLE         INVENTORY
                      CO-AD               SYSTEM             BILLING
                      ECS                                    ECS
```

```
INVENTORY MANAGEMENT

SALES INFORMATION          EDI                              P.O.S.T.
                           TRANSACTION

SALES BUDGET               BUDGET/FORECAST                  ACCOUNTS PAYABLE SYSTEM
PROCESS                    (COMSHARE)                       (JDE)
----------
FORECAST
P.S.I.
```

```
A C C O U N T I N G   S Y S T E M  (JDE)
```

```
ELECTRONIC OFFICE COMMUNICATION
```

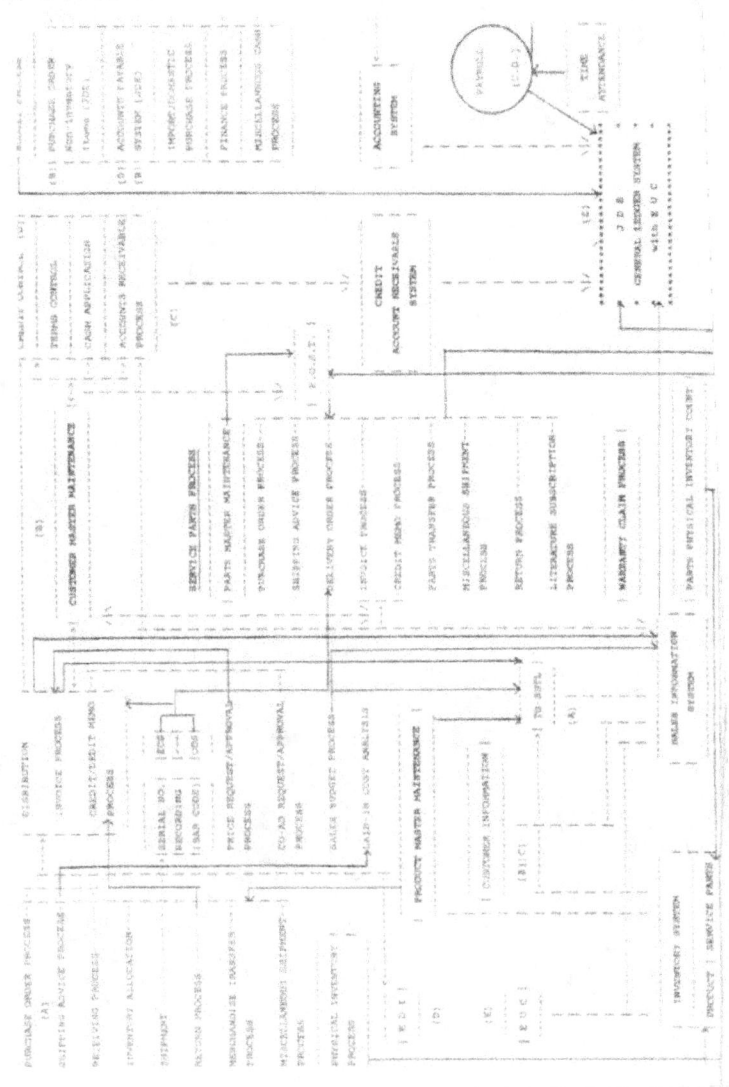

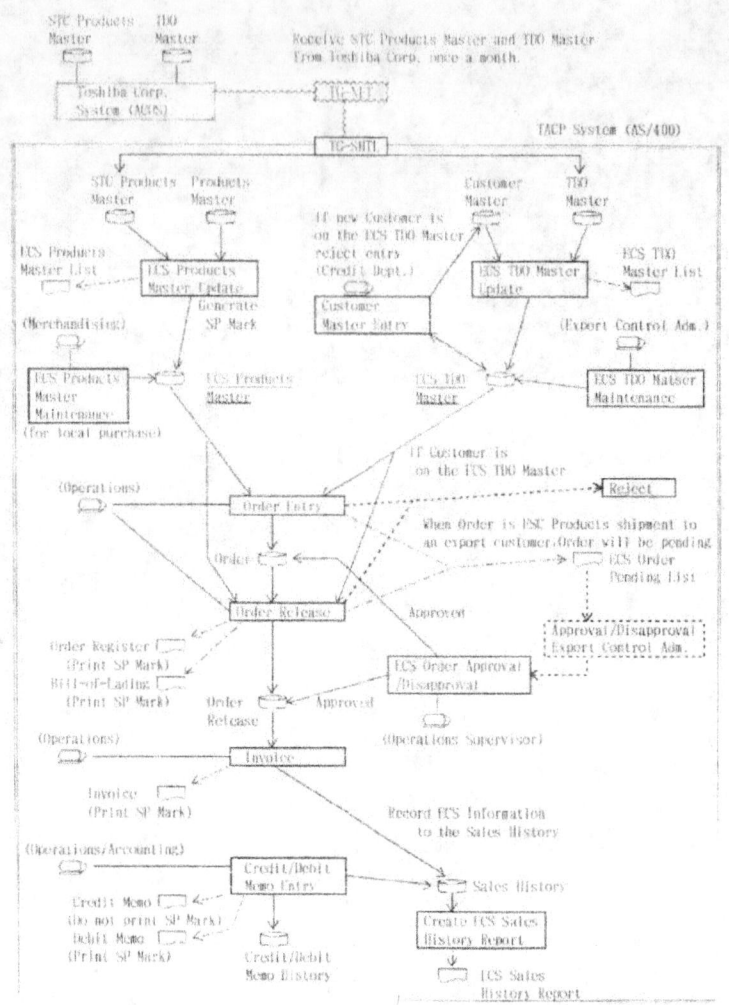

Export Control System

Data Communication Network

TAI/TACP operations evolved their data communication from overnight mail delivery of punched cards from the Los Angeles Sales Branch to dial-up batch data transfer from the Los Angeles and Chicago Sales Branches, online data transfer from seven sales branches with public telephone lines, and online data entry via T1, packet networks, and frame relay/token-ring. Individual PC users were supported through client-server and Internet communication.

Public telephone lines were not ready to service dial-up communication in 1970. Data transfers were frequently disconnected in the middle of the transactions due to noise interference. Operating a notebook PC attached to a modem for dial-up connection was almost impossible because of noise disturbances on public telephone lines. T1 connections gave TAI proper online operation, but the operation of multiple-line connections was not cost-effective.

When Kiyoshi began considering the introduction of a packet network, he interviewed a few network providers. AT&T offered the most aggressive presentation because the company was a latecomer to the packet network service provider business. AT&T promised its complete support for the successful installation of a packet network for TAI, assigning a sales engineer who had been involved in developing packet networks at Bell Laboratories. Kiyoshi decided to install a packet network from AT&T. It proved to be the right decision, as AT&T had promised to work around the clock to fix any glitches. The installation was done on time and successfully.

AT&T took divestiture action while TACP was in the midst of conversion from the packet network to frame relay. People who were working for TACP from AT&T could not support TACP continuously because they would be assigned to other areas due to its reorganization. The group of people from AT&T working with TACP was quite knowledgeable about the company's operations. If a new crew from AT&T was assigned to TACP during the conversion from packet network to frame relay network, it would take a lot longer to complete the installation. Kiyoshi consulted the Legal Department again and chose, at this time, to send a letter to the Legal Department at AT&T Headquarters protesting any crew changes. He emphasized that changing AT&T members assigned to TACP would damage the business practices of the company. The Branch Manager of AT&T visited Kiyoshi within a week, stating that there would be no change of assignment of current AT&T staff to TACP , no matter what happened to AT&T's divestiture action.

External PC access to TACP was protected by firewalls, but one concern was that if anyone brought their own PC with a virus and connected it to TACP's LAN, the virus could spread to other PCs used by LAN users. PC specialists in the Information Systems Department were constantly monitoring the LAN and its users to solve any problems. These dedicated people were taking their responsibilities seriously.

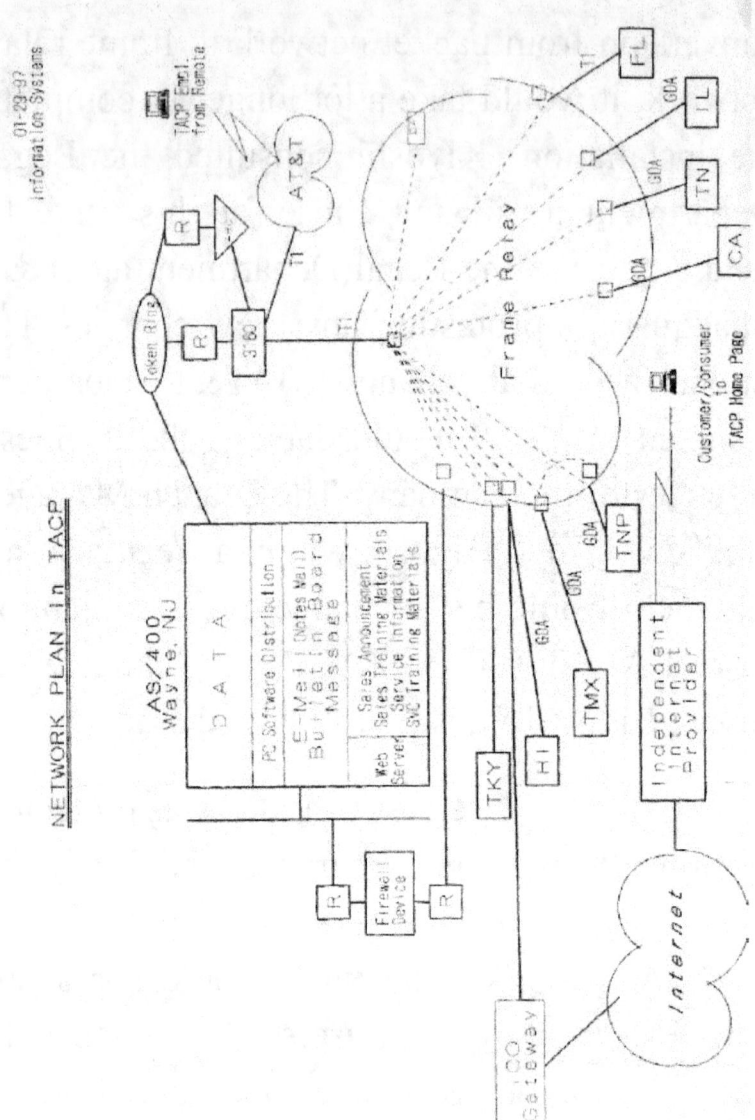

NETWORK PLAN in TACP

01-29-97
Information Systems

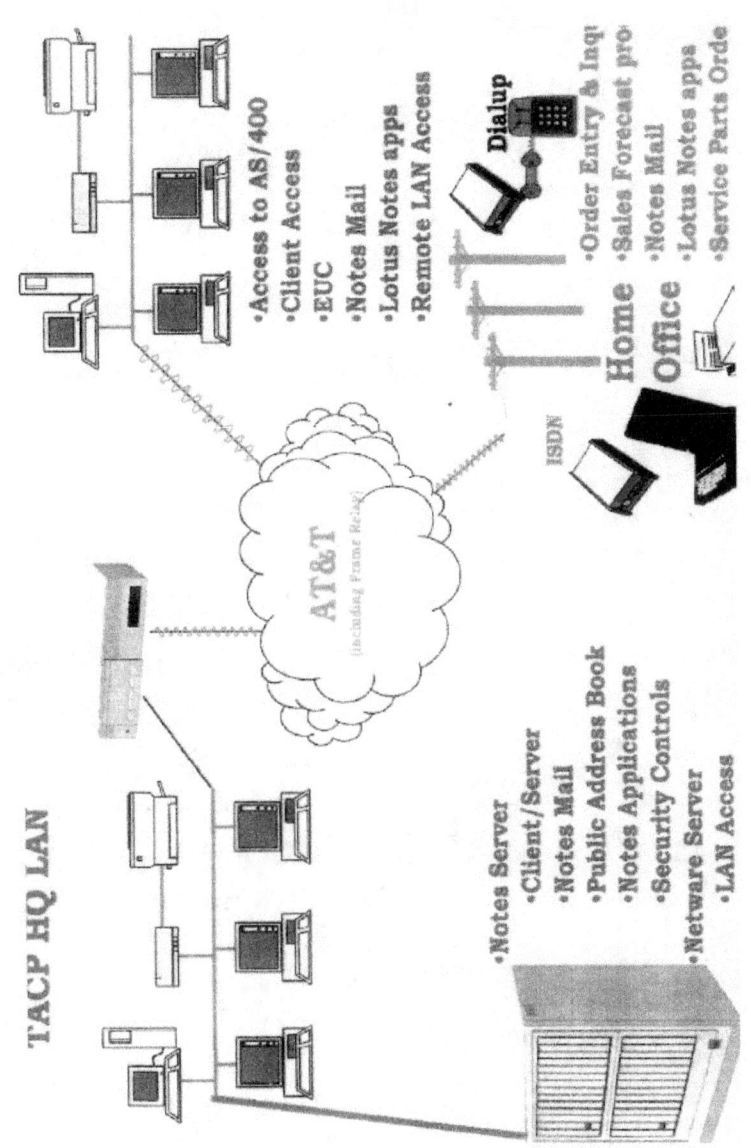

TACP HQ LAN

- Notes Server
  - Client/Server
  - Notes Mail
  - Public Address Book
  - Notes Applications
  - Security Controls
- Netware Server
  - LAN Access

AT&T
(Including Frame Relay)

ISDN

Home
Office

Dialup

- Access to AS/400
- Client Access
- EUC
- Notes Mail
- Lotus Notes apps
- Remote LAN Access

- Order Entry & Inq
- Sales Forecast pro
- Notes Mail
- Lotus Notes apps
- Service Parts Orde

175

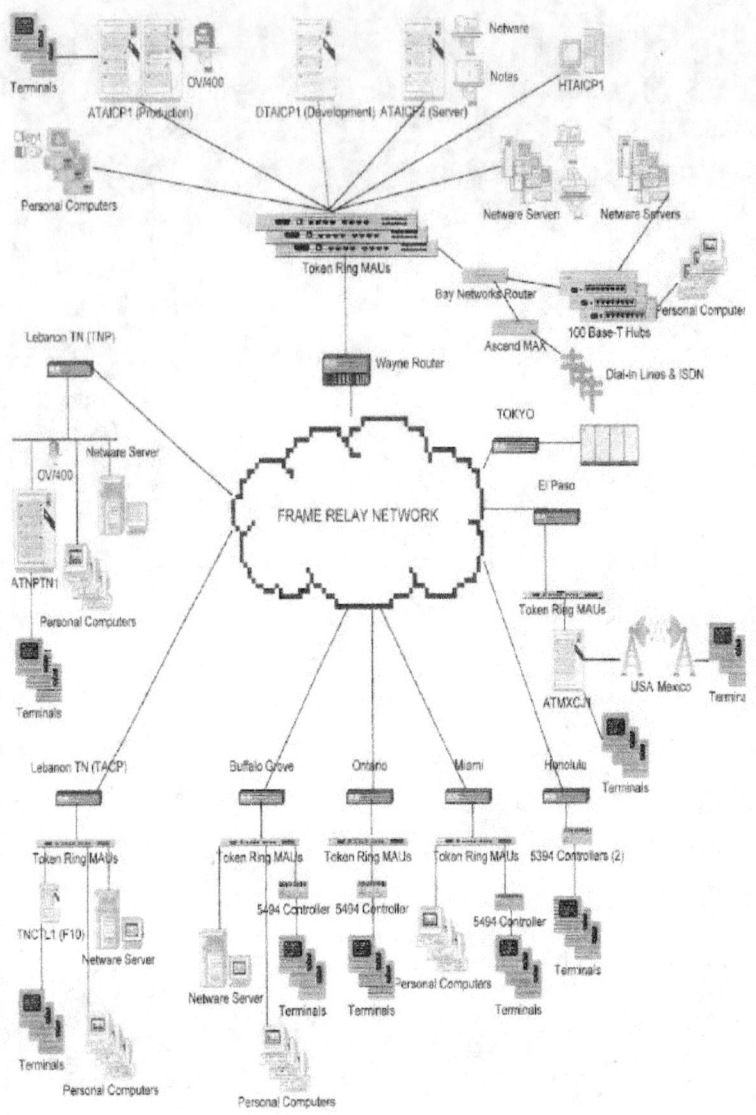

Project Management

There were four kinds of information systems projects to manage:

1. System user requirements: application programs, client-server related

2. System interface requirements from external organizations: EDI, data exchange interfaces with the Toshiba group, and data communication security

3. Support for personal computer users: hardware/software preparation, data communication with security considerations, PC interfaces with the system database, and internet connection

4. Information systems operations: system upgrades (hardware/software), system maintenance, system conceptual study and change, daily operations, data network maintenance, and its upgrades

The Information Systems Department undertook projects that involved internal information systems operations, which were scheduled and managed by the department alone. When system users were involved, the Information Systems Department needed to define the proceedings for establishing projects with all related user departments. The initial discussion with the system user requester led to a shared understanding of the scope of the project. Internal discussion in the Information Systems Department led to assigning members of the project team and establishing an estimated delivery date for the required system to the system users. This teamwork included time for system design, application programming, system availability, data communication considerations, system documentation, and user documentation. The Information Systems Department presented its proposal to the system user representative to finalize the project plan. The Information Systems Department retained responsibility for meeting the presented system delivery date promised to the system requester. This delivery date was subject to change if system users modified the project contents. System user management signed off on the project at the time of system delivery. Post-installation follow-ups would then proceed. Procedural project management is illustrated as follows.

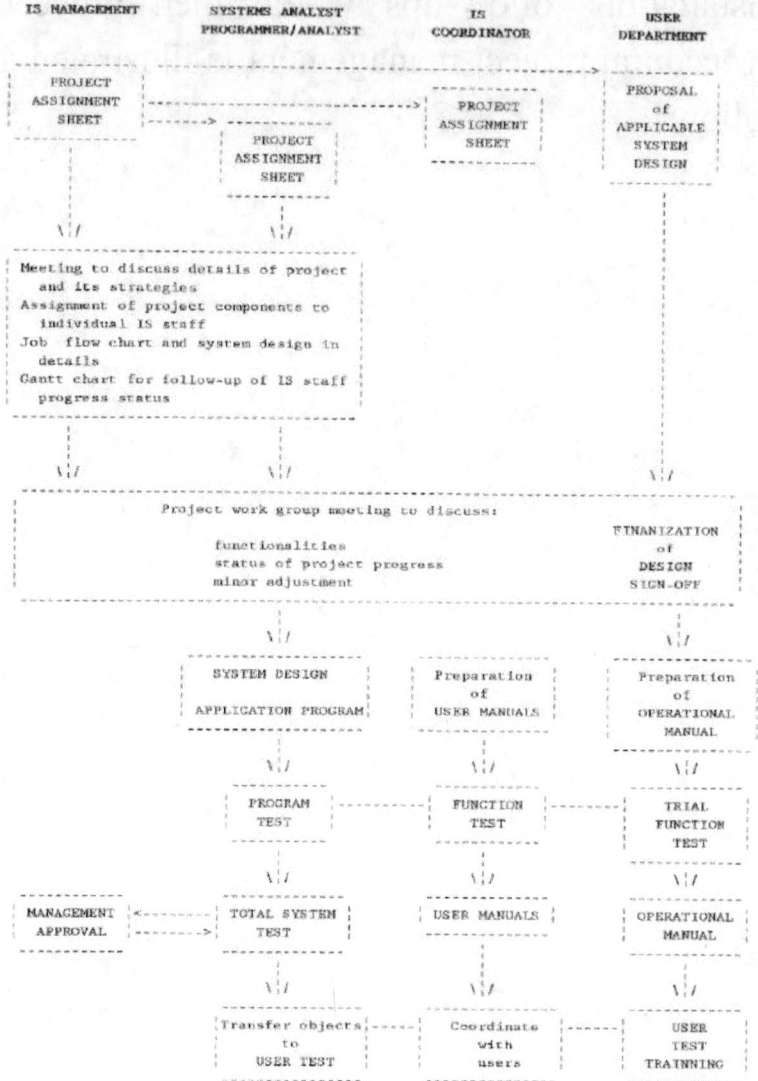

IS MANAGEMENT	SYSTEMS ANALYST PROGRAMMER/ANALYST	IS COORDINATOR	USER DEPARTMENT

Meeting with users to discuss:

        the result of testing
        minor adjustment
        final decision of system implementation

MANAGEMENT APPROVAL	Transfer objects to PRODUCTION LIB.	USER MANUALS	USER MANUALS

Post installation meeting with users to discuss:

        condition of installation
        minor adjustment if necessary

MANAGEMENT APPROVAL	Complete PROJECT ASSIGNMENT SHEET		

| | | IS ACTIVITY REPORT | SIGN-OFF of PROJECT |

FILE   FILE

181

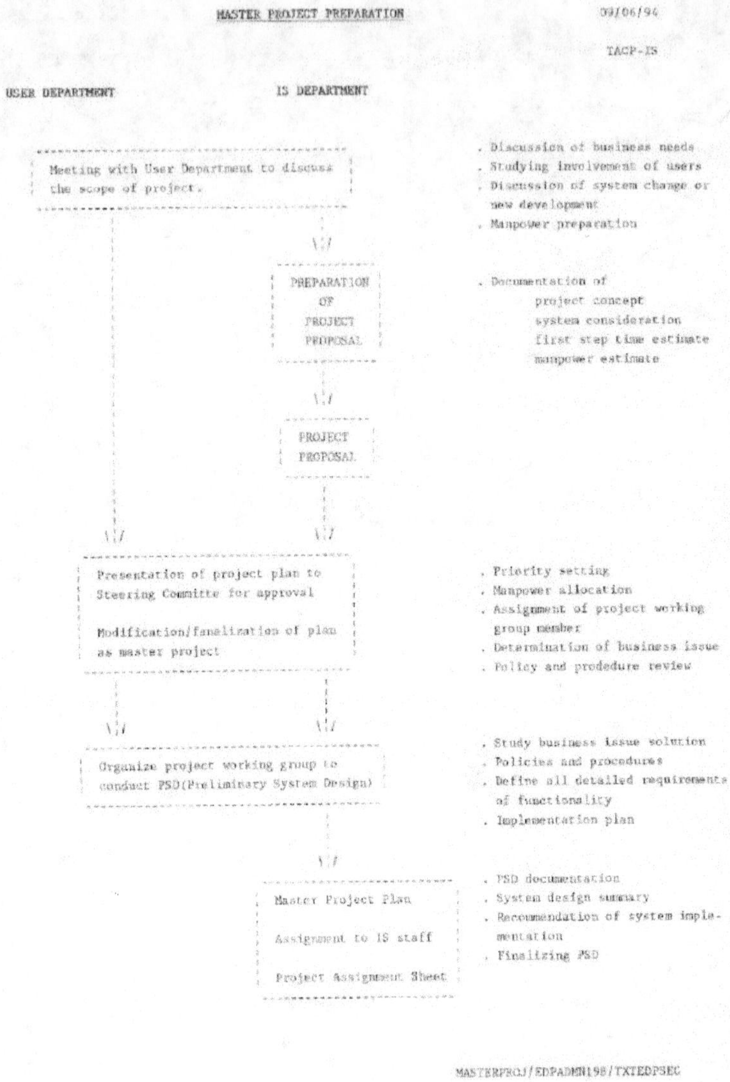

MASTER PROJECT PREPARATION
09/06/94
TACP-IS
USER DEPARTMENT
IS DEPARTMENT
Meeting with User Department to discuss the scope of project.
. Discussion of business needs
. Studying involvement of users
. Discussion of system change or new development
. Manpower preparation
PREPARATION OF PROJECT PROPOSAL
. Documentation of
project concept
system consideration
first step time estimate
manpower estimate
PROJECT PROPOSAL
Presentation of project plan to Steering Committe for approval
Modification/finalization of plan as master project
. Priority setting
. Manpower allocation
. Assignment of project working group member
. Determination of business issue
. Policy and prodedure review
Organize project working group to conduct PSD(Preliminary System Design)
. Study business issue solution
. Policies and procedures
. Define all detailed requirements of functionality
. Implementation plan
Master Project Plan
Assignment to IS staff
Project Assignment Sheet
. PSD documentation
. System design summary
. Recommendation of system implementation
. Finalizing PSD
MASTERPROJ/EDPADMN198/TXTEDPSEC

When the concept of the project was defined, project management organized its team, introduced the project, requested the deadline, assigned jobs to each member of the team, and analyzed system capability and data communication network availability. Project Management requested that the team start preparing their delivery estimate after an open discussion of potential issues. When they were ready to present their estimated delivery date, Project Management called for a meeting of all team members to have an open discussion of ideas and difficulties. Each member contributed solutions to help finalize the project on time. This practice encouraged team members and drew on the full range of their abilities. Collective responsibility and individual contributions to the team motivated them to work more effectively and increased their satisfaction with the project.

Project Management handled multiple projects at once. It was like spinning multiple saucers; it was a nerve-racking responsibility. There was no perfect work; projects were always subject to question. The testing system was conducted from the system user's point of view instead of the system developer's. System developers worked in virtual data environments to simulate the exact production concept. The user manual developer examined the system from the system user's point of view before releasing the completed system to the production side, which was separated by a partition in the computer.

Project Management constantly checked ongoing projects at the interim stage of their development. Requests for modification of system applications by system user management had to be examined by Project Management to determine the feasibility of requested modifications. Project members of the Information Systems Department shared all issues related to changes and problems under the supervision of Project Management.

When a member of the project team had difficulty proceeding with their work or had constructive ideas, Kiyoshi gathered the project members for a short meeting to share these issues and seek conclusions to keep the project running. These issues were personal, technical, scheduling-related, or the result of disagreements between team members. The most important consideration for Project Management was that the Information Systems Department put forth every effort to maintain the delivery schedule once it was published. Project members in the Information Systems Department shared collective responsibility for completing every system delivery to the system users on time.

Information Systems Management and Operations

System planning (software and hardware, daily system operations), staying updated on developments in the information systems industry, and managing Information Systems personnel were all part of system operations. It was a challenge for Information Systems Management to continually update its capabilities. Information Systems Management was expected to prepare for foreseeable technological advancements in response to increasingly advanced future applications required by system user management.

Almost all the system fixes, maintenance, and system upgrades were executed outside normal business hours. The Information Systems Department worked late at night and on weekends to complete its work, if necessary. Dedicated Information Systems members were willing to spend extra time, including weekends, to complete their goals. Vendors like IBM and AT&T cooperated by sending their engineers and service people. Kiyoshi usually attended the work sessions in case the team needed additional vendor specialists to solve unexpected problems. He would contact Vendor Management to request prompt dispatch of the proper personnel. Kiyoshi's participation usually worked well to ensure tasks were completed on time. As far as daily system operations were concerned, the Information Systems Department never disturbed the work of system users by any means, thanks to its preventive measures.

Members of the Information Systems Department absorbed updated system-related information from industrial publications and attended various seminars. Kiyoshi not only attended seminars and events for information systems executives; he was also invited by AT&T to visit Bell Laboratories and the international network control center. IBM invited him on a day trip by corporate jet to three locations. The first trip was to the AS/400 manufacturing plant in Rochester, Minnesota. The second day trip was to the semiconductor manufacturing plant in Vermont, which also produced 32-bit chips for CPUs. A 32-bit CPU chip was the most advanced processor used in the AS/400. The third day trip was to the personal computer manufacturing plant in Boca Raton, Florida.

One day, Kiyoshi received a phone call. The caller introduced himself as a representative of the Aspen Institute and invited Kiyoshi to join the Forum for Information Executives. Kiyoshi was unsure whether the caller was real. The caller offered to send him the program agenda and other materials by mail. A package was delivered the next day, and Kiyoshi realized that the invitation was valid. It was a week-long forum held at the River House in the Wye Center in Maryland, conducted by the Institute for Information Studies. Another phone call came from the same person the next day to confirm that Kiyoshi had received the mail. Kiyoshi then accepted the invitation.

He arrived at Baltimore/Washington International Airport on May 18, 1992, as scheduled. A limousine was waiting outside the baggage claim area and took him to the River House Conference Center. The first day's session started the next morning. The twenty-six participants consisted of ten professors from universities all over the US, several government personnel, corporate executives, a business consultant, and representatives from nonprofit organizations. The program focused on organization, information technology, open discussion, and case studies. Kiyoshi relished expressing his opinion in every session, confirming that his way of managing Information Systems was moving the company in the right direction. He also called attention to analytical methods. Lengthy descriptive reports commonly used in the business community did not emphasize the focal point enough. Kyoshi advocated for the use of matrix charts—describing all issues versus solving problems.

Toward the end of the week-long session, the forum presented a case study on how mid-sized business entities should run under crucial situations. The forum chair assigned five participants to a group to work on the case. Kiyoshi was assigned to a group with a professor from Harvard University, a business consultant, and two other executives. When they began working on the case, they asked Kiyoshi to make a matrix chart. He thought about how to handle the situation and told the group that they should use the matrix since he brought it to the class. He wanted to watch how they would do it. They worked intensely on matrix charts to finish the case. His group was awarded first place among the five groups. Kiyoshi was delighted to have these intellectual discussions. His time at the Forum confirmed that he was working in the right direction in Information Systems Management.

Budget Management

The business of consumer electronics was highly competitive in the United States. TACP had struggled to maintain a positive Profit/Loss Result (PLR). On the other hand, TACP's management aggressively focused on increasing its revenue. Sales programs became more complicated to keep pace with up to twenty competitors.

The Information Systems Department tried to accommodate the request for more complex distribution systems from Sales/Marketing Management. The budget of the Information Systems Department in the US was usually related to the company's revenue rather than P/L. Most US companies allocated an average budget for Information Systems of 1–2 % of the company's revenue. In contrast, TACP allowed less than 0.2 % of its revenue. Top management claimed that they could not afford to match the level of US companies' budgets for Information Systems operations due to the P/L situation. It was no use arguing with them since top management was only interested in sales activities.

Kiyoshi put in the effort to match the Information Systems Department's payroll with US market standards and minimize the expense of system operations. He negotiated with leasing companies to handle operating system software and hardware replacements or updates within lease terms, based on their residual value. These contracts gave TACP more flexibility and helped minimize expenses.

When it came to installing a new system or communication network, Kiyoshi negotiated with vendors to complete the installation without any consulting fees. They were willing to install systems or communication networks without additional engineering support fees for TACP because it was usually a pioneering installation among their customers. They could refer them to others, using this as an example of successful operations.

As to the payroll system, Kiyoshi had no intention of being involved because the nature of the data was too sensitive to be managed by the Information Systems Department.

The Information Systems Department in the Tennessee manufacturing plant used a commercial manufacturing application package that included a payroll system. A manager in the Information Systems Department complained to Kiyoshi when she found out that she was underpaid compared to other managers by looking up payroll records in the database. This was the exact reason Kiyoshi did not want to be involved with the payroll system at TACP.

Personnel Management

Every member of the Information Systems Department was professional and dedicated to their work. The most important consideration was maintaining confidence in their professionalism. Sharing information, paying attention to policies/procedures, understanding the scope of the project, receiving clear job assignments, providing self-estimates for assignment completion, and problem-solving as a team contributed to effective work by the team. A total of twenty-six members in the Information Systems Department was not enough to accomplish all the necessary tasks. Kiyoshi encouraged everyone to challenge themselves to the best of their abilities.

Headhunters constantly contacted members of the Information Systems Department, offering better jobs and better pay, but most chose to stay at TACP. They liked the way everyone shared responsibility and had open discussions, working together as a team. Members of the Information Systems Department were not rewarded like salespeople, who received annual bonuses according to their sales achievements. Kiyoshi instead emphasized professional rewards when the projects were completed on time.

All members of the Information Systems Department were familiar with every system, and all work was documented. The project team became capable, without Kiyoshi's guidance, of handling the evaluation of work, estimating delivery times for projects, enacting quality control, delivering the system to users, and assisting system users with written manuals.

A semi-annual evaluation of personnel in the department was based on technical skills, effective teamwork, self-motivating ability, and completing assigned work on time.

Arthur Andersen System Consulting conducted audits of Information Systems operations as an independent contractor. The Information Systems Division of Toshiba Corp. also underwent a separate internal audit. Both audit reports on the Information Systems Department advised the President of TACP to increase the number of staff and the budget for the department to meet the scope of its operations. The allocation of 0.2% of TACP's revenue was too low for the scope of operation of the Information Systems Department. No other negative comments were reported.

Maintaining ethical conduct was not popular among the rest of the people in TACP. Other employees looked at members of the Information Systems Department as being too square. Kiyoshi encouraged them to stand firm when it came to professionalism. Personal standards may differ from those in other departments.

Part VI

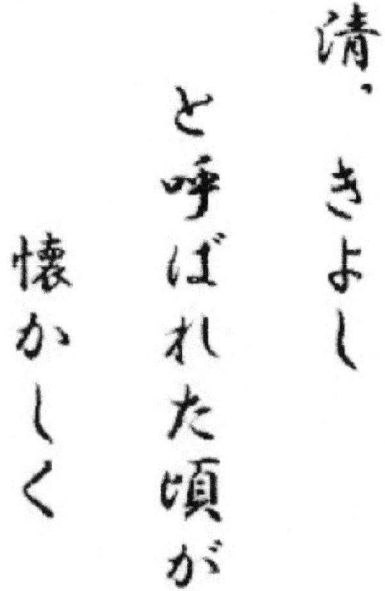

Kiyoshi, Kiyoshi

When I was called

nostalgia

I missed the living in those days she called to
me— "Kiyoshi… Kiyoshi."

CHAPTER 10
Preparation for Retirement

Kiyoshi was struggling to see what life was all about. Studying in school, working at Toshiba, and associating with friends may all be a part of life. But what was the real goal? What about the relationship between body and soul? What was his hope for his life?

Kyoshi saw school as preparation for his future. Working at Toshiba was preparation to reach financial goals. He, in the meantime, handled anything coming at him as a challenge to his ability and worked to get the maximum possible result. However, his satisfaction was not with that kind of life. He felt he might still be preparing to reach his real life. Receiving paychecks from the workplace and being paid for business trips were part of his job, yet he was not a free agent in his life. Managing the Information Systems Department was the only job Kiyoshi was able to do at TAI/TACP that maintained his clear conscience. Some people expected Kiyoshi to take on more executive management responsibilities. The Chairman of TAI proposed that Kiyoshi become CIO. Kiyoshi declined his offer. He wanted to concentrate on working in Information Systems, not to be involved in internal politics. He did not want to compromise his conscience.

Kiyoshi surmised that Toshiba/TACP was reaching the peak of its business. Outsourcing consumer products to manufacturers in foreign countries and closing its own manufacturing plants in Japan, the US, Mexico, and elsewhere did not promise success for TACP. Toshiba instead positioned TACP as a trading firm.

When Kiyoshi reached age sixty, he realized that his mind was not as agile as it used to be. He was still able to contend with the necessary work, but it required more concentration. He thought now was the time to face his real life and do everything together with Charlotte, his lifelong companion. He applied for US citizenship at the US Emigration Office in 1997, which caused him to lose his Japanese citizenship since the Japanese government did not allow dual citizenship. This status change simplified legal issues, allowing him not to be involved in any Japanese laws. He began looking toward retirement, finding a successor to continue operating Information Systems at TACP. Members of the Information Systems Department became capable of managing information systems, and everything else was documented.

CHAPTER 11
Life After Retirement

Kiyoshi retired from TACP on May 1, 1998, when top management found his successor. The president requested Kiyoshi to remain as a senior advisor with pay for at least six months. Kiyoshi agreed to stay with no pay, but with possession of the company automobiles, which he had been using, and a top-of-the-line Toshiba notebook PC.

Charlotte was delighted to plan their future life together. They had their twenty-fifth silver anniversary event. Then they started talking about their fiftieth golden anniversary. Kiyoshi finally found out what life was about—pleasing his companion and doing everything together without any disturbances. Any problems that came to them could be contended with together.

Greeted by Charlotte's friend in Vienna, Austria

Dinner with Kaneko, Ikeno families in Tokyo

Lunch at the temple in Nara

Dinner after wedding of Kiyoshi's niece at the International House of Japan

Charlotte at Kiyomizu Temple

Dinner at Ryokan

Toshiba International Information Systems Seminar 1985

God made men and women for the purpose of not only producing offspring but also pleasing each other with four kinds of love: principal, friendship, romantic, and charitable. Charlotte and Kiyoshi took pleasure in these loves. This was the real meaning of life. The only problem he still could not resolve was the issue of "body and soul." If death brings the end of a body, then what causes the end of the soul?

In the meantime, Charlotte scouted out ideas for traveling and Kiyoshi materialized a travel itinerary to Europe, Japan, Maine to Florida, and the West Coast by car, airline, and train (Amtrak). They loved the fact that they paid all expenses from their pocket money—no one assisted them in planning or paid for these travels.

Charlotte encouraged Kiyoshi to write his autobiography. Kiyoshi had been scribbling, gathering memories of his past—from childhood to the end of his professional career—just for his personal interest. It took him almost ten years to complete the work. It was an enjoyable time, with Charlotte encouraging Kyoshi to work together on planning to convert it into a manuscript for a book. Proofreading began after Kiyoshi typed it in book format using Microsoft Word. One of Charlotte's friends recommended that Kiyoshi write a book and introduced him to a printing company she always used for her own books (she had written seven).

When they finished writing, they came up with a title for the book, a design for the book cover, and a final manuscript, which they copied onto a CD. They then visited the printing company in Schenectady, New York. After numerous visits and communications by telephone and email, *KH in Seven Decades* was completed. The printing company recommended and pursued obtaining an ISBN and registering the book with the Library of Congress.

In the meantime, Charlotte and Kiyoshi consolidated the poems Charlotte had written since high school. Kiyoshi organized her collection into a book format. Charlotte struggled to finalize it because it was difficult for her to concentrate due to her weakening health. Kiyoshi finished printing the book after Charlotte had passed.

Charlotte was interested in the local history of Sussex County, where she and Kiyoshi lived. She asked Kiyoshi to accompany her on visits to the Sussex County Historical Society. One of the trustees approached Charlotte, after several visits there, and asked her to become a member of the Board of Trustees since he recognized her father's ancestor (going back to a few generations) as one of the emigrants on the Mayflower from

England. Charlotte turned around, pointing at Kiyoshi, and said he was the one who should be a trustee. Kiyoshi hesitated at first, but Charlotte firmly insisted, so he gave in.

The Sussex County Historical Society was established in 1906, and its museum building is listed in the National Register as the oldest existing historical museum building in the state of New Jersey. Its collection includes locally discovered mastodon bones and ivory, the remains of Indigenous people, agricultural pioneering items, artifacts from the Revolutionary and Civil Wars, items from World Wars I and II, information about old local businesses, a registry of former residents in the county, and more.

Kiyoshi was not interested in becoming a historian, but he realized that the Society was administratively under capacity; the Constitution and bylaws were not written practically, historical documents were scattered all over the storage area, and the inventory of historical collections had not been recorded.

He began designing and creating documents for all business transactions: receipt forms, gift agreements, sales agreements, lending and loan agreements, volunteer agreements, applications for use of the Society's facilities, and applications for trustees.

Some forms were verified by an attorney for legal issues. Kyoshi made an operational procedural document for the Society's museum and provided internal accounting procedures and an accounting system. He gathered all documents into a binder and named it the Black Book and distributed copies to all trustees.

The Society's President wanted to work with Kiyoshi alone to rewrite the bylaws, but Kiyoshi preferred teamwork. Five members, including the President, began the work of rewriting the bylaws from scratch. One of Kiyoshi's biggest concerns was the role of the executives. The President insisted on exercising his authority, but Kiyoshi said that the executives were there to serve the Society. The finalized bylaws were a result of compromise, but they were much better than the previous ones. All trustees voted to implement the new bylaws.

In the meantime, Kiyoshi began listing the historical collections' items from the gift document files. Then two other members joined to take a physical inventory of the collection, moving from room to room. The inventory documents were compiled in list form, in a binder four inches thick.

Kiyoshi realized there was no historic site map of the entire Sussex County, though some township-level maps existed. He proposed creating a county-wide historic sites map during a Board of Trustees meeting held in preparation of the Society's centennial event. All Board members agreed with Kiyoshi's idea, but nobody offered to work on it. Kiyoshi initiated the gathering of information: historical sites registered in the National Register, local registrations by the county and townships, historical documents, and books. Local historians were mostly limited to knowledge of their own townships. There are twenty-four municipalities in Sussex County, and Kiyoshi compiled descriptions of each township, as well as of Sussex County—how it started and its characteristics—and sent them to each township for verification. He began assembling the map: labels for historic sites, street numbers by county and NJ state, historic site photos, streets and railroads, and checking with local historians for the correct locations of the sites. It was tedious work.

A handmade historic site map was on the front, with descriptions of twenty-four individual municipalities and other statistical information on the back—the handmade map was completed. The Society invited all local historians to the museum to verify Kyoshi's handmade historic site map before it was approved for printing. There was no printing facility capable of CAD processing in Sussex County, so Kiyoshi, with the help of his friend, contacted a printing company in Bernardsville, New Jersey. Kiyoshi provided them with a CD containing labels for historic sites, street numbers, photos of historic sites, descriptions of twenty-four municipalities, and other information, along with the handmade historic site map. He requested that the printing company use all information from the CD exactly as it is.

After numerous rounds of collaboration with the printing company, Kiyoshi received the map on the very day of the Centennial Day celebration. Copies of the map were handed out to people who attended the event. Kiyoshi obtained an ISBN and registered the map with the Library of Congress. It took him three years to complete the work. The *Jersey Herald* (a local newspaper) wrote an article introducing the Sussex County Historic Site Map, covering more than a full page.

Kiyoshi confirmed each subject he worked on during Board of Trustees meetings. He submitted progress reports of his work to gain consensus before moving on to the next step. This way, everyone on the Board was informed before anything became official.

A member of the Board of Trustees wanted Kiyoshi to serve as Parliamentarian. Kiyoshi was reluctant to accept the position because, as the Parliamentarian, he would not have voting rights at Board meetings according to Robert's Rules. The Board of Trustees modified the bylaws and established a position for the Parliamentarian with voting rights and a member of the Executive Committee. In light of these changes, Kiyoshi had no reason to decline the offer , so he accepted the responsibility.

He realized that everything had become routine, and most of the trustees did not follow the rules and regulations established in the bylaws anyway. He decided it was time to leave the Society and move on to a different way of life. He submitted his Letter of Resignation to the Board after having been a member for five years. A friend advised Kiyoshi to join the Rotary Club and introduced him to the President of the Vernon chapter. Afterward, Kiyoshi decided to become a member there.

Charlotte started losing her health. Whenever Kiyoshi went to his medical doctors, she always accompanied him. His doctors observed Charlotte's health situation. They offered to examine her physical condition, but she declined their offer. She finally told Kiyoshi that she would go to the Cleveland Clinic in Orlando, Florida. He made an appointment at the Clinic and made a reservation for a hotel located next to the Clinic. When they started to walk from the hotel to the reception desk of the Clinic the next morning, she suddenly changed her mind and refused to admit herself.

Charlotte's physical situation was progressively worsening to the point that it was hard for her to walk. She asked Kiyoshi to take her to the Chamber Music Concert at the Wilmington Hotel in Wilmington, Delaware, which they had attended seasonally. Kiyoshi had to use the hotel's wheelchair to carry Charlotte into the concert hall. That was the last occasion they went out together.

Charlotte could not get out of bed after they returned home from the concert. She still refused to go to the doctor over the next two weeks. Then, she finally gave in and asked Kiyoshi to take her to a hospital. Kiyoshi immediately arranged a private ambulance to take her to Morristown Memorial Hospital for emergency admission. Kiyoshi stayed overnight with Charlotte in her hospital room for a month and a half until the end of her life. Twenty years of post-retirement life, the most fruitful part of life for Kiyoshi, had come to an end.

After the funeral and legal matters were completed, Kiyoshi felt as though he were losing his mind. He forgot the directions to where he was driving at night. He broke dishes when he was washing them. He decided to take a trip to clear his head. He rented an apartment in Tokyo for three months. His friends took him on a trip to Kiyosato in Yamanashi Prefecture, where he stayed overnight. Kiyoshi also spent time with his family and friends in Tokyo.

Living in Japan for three months successfully shifted his state of mind. He was able to sustain his single life, which was not ideal but is now tolerable. Memories of happiness with Charlotte and doing everything together remained in Kiyoshi's mind.

As for Charlotte's parents, her father passed away in 1998. Her mother went to an assisted living facility in her hometown after living alone for several years. Charlotte and Kiyoshi visited her once a month, except when they traveled. Kiyoshi continued to visit her after Charlotte had passed. Since Charlotte was an only child and most of her mother's immediate relatives were gone, he took care of Charlotte's mother's needs and served as an Executor with Power of Attorney until the end of her life at ninety-seven years old.

It is Kiyoshi's greatest challenge to pursue living his remaining life alone. He must face the reality of being a single man. But life is sweet, and it is bitter. It all depends on how he chooses to handle it.

わが妻は
那辺の何処か
我知らず

My eternal companion

Where ever you are

I do not know

I do not know where you are.